"I have long believed that retailers, enthralled by supply chain innovations and enraptured by technological disruptions, often lose sight of the people for whom everything should be targeted: customers. Gary Hawkins, in "Retail in the Age of 'I'," does a compelling job of bringing the focus back where it belongs. It is about building relationships, not just sales; it is about understanding the importance of lifetime customer value, not just the size of individual transactions. Gary long has been a prophet, but with this new book, he gives his evangelical fervor new depth, and yet makes it applicable, relevant, and perhaps most important, resonant. This is a must-read for retailers looking to thrive in a cutthroat 21st century retail environment."

- Kevin Coupe, "Content Guy, "MorningNewsBeat.com"

As an executive with relevant experience across the retail industry spectrum, Gary is uniquely positioned to opine on the innovation imperative facing retail today. His focus on the "i" is exactly what's needed to help retailers compete in an increasingly disrupted environment, and his call to action evokes a sixth "i" – "Inspiring."

- Patrick Spear
President & CEO
Global Market Development Center

"Retail in the Age of i' outlines the innovation imperative in retail today--Gary is absolutely right in calling for retailers to wake up to the 'utter disruption' happening in every corner of the industry. This book will help readers in the retail industry understand the issues they should be thinking about and help them prepare for the massive shifts on the horizon."

- Zia Daniell Widger
Chief Global Content Officer, Shoptalk
Co-Founder, Groceryshop

"How does a retailer get a good night's sleep in today's reality of disruption and intense technology and data-driven competition? Gary Hawkins' Retail in the Age of 'i' will not solve retailers' insomnia but it will help them "know more about what they don't know". Hawkins combines his deep experience in the supermarket business with his passion for customer data-driven analytics and insights to clearly explain how retailers can use new technologies and capabilities to build relationships with the right customers."

- Charles J. Skuba
Senior Associate Dean for Custom Executive Education
Professor of the Practice
International Business and International Marketing
Georgetown University McDonough School of Business

Gary Hawkins is one of the true treasures of our industry. His knowledge of industry issues and solution sets when combined with deep operational experience and technology savvy yields a perspective that is completely unique. The result is thought leadership at the highest levels delivering both insight and practicality. This book is a must read for those retailers wishing to both understand and thrive in the Age of "i".

- Lance Jacobs
Vice President, Personalized Wellness
ScriptSave

Retail in the Age of

A New Worldview for the
Retail Industry

GARY E. HAWKINS

Retail in the Age of 'i'

ISBN: 9781796614817

Hawkins, Gary E.
Retail in the Age of 'i'

Published by: Retail Mindsteps, LLC

Dedication

To my wife Heather, for her loving support and constant
encouragement.

And to my growing family -

Sterling,
Berkeley, Sasha, Madeline, and Isabelle,
Schuyler
&
Haviland

May you all live long and prosper!

Contents

"The best way to predict the future is to create it."

Abraham Lincoln

Preface

May you live in interesting times. My life has been, and continues to be, an embodiment of that expression.

I grew up on in my family's grocery store, learning from an early age the importance of cleanliness, high-quality fresh foods, and customer service. The importance of the customer is a mantra that still resonates after many years.

Around this same time, the science fiction I loved to read was making its way from the printed page to the screen in our living room, and the even bigger screen at the local movie theater. It's pretty wild today to see Isaac Asimov's robots becoming a reality, conversing with Alexa as a modern-day Hal of 2001 A Space Odyssey, and watching 3D food printing emulate the replicator on board Star Trek's USS Enterprise.

I attended high school when computer programming was just beginning to be recognized as a valuable skill; I remember taking a course in Basic programming and having to write a simple program on a terminal in the school's office tied to a mainframe at a nearby university. That early interest in computers continued when I purchased one of the original Mac computers when they first appeared in 1984, not really knowing what I was going to do with it but sure the machine would be transformative.

I also experienced firsthand many changes in retail growing up in my family's supermarket and wholesale business. I helped install our first scanning POS system in the late 1970s, gaining appreciation for the importance of data.

My belief in the transformative power of technology in the retail industry took hold when I started one of the first frequent shopper programs in the U.S. supermarket industry in early 1993, driven by a powerful instinct that customer data would be a game changer and help an independent grocer go up against some of the best retailers in the business.

I was in the right place at the right time to lead a good deal of early industry learning about true customer behavior, shopper-level economics, and more, growing from the new world of customer-identified purchase data. That early work triggered successive waves of innovation that continue to this day. Over the years I have been privileged to work with leading companies in the retail industry around the world, including the likes of Kroger, Mitsubishi, Procter & Gamble, Unilever, and many others.

Throughout this time we leveraged my family's store as a laboratory, testing and trialing not only new marketing concepts but, increasingly, new technologies. For the past two decades I have become increasingly convinced of the importance of technology to transform retail. And this belief continues today. Seeing the coming explosion in new innovation, we formed CART - the Center for Advancing Retail & Technology - several years ago to help retailers learn about and make sense of new technologies flooding into the market.

CART today sits at the epicenter of fast moving consumer goods (FMCG) retail innovation, currently reviewing over 1,000 new capabilities coming into the industry each year and providing services to retailers, wholesalers, brand manufacturers, and solution providers as transformation accelerates across the supply chain.

Needless to say, I've seen more change in the past few years than my father did in his lifetime.

And change is speeding up everywhere. When I published my first book nearly twenty years ago it involved sending the manuscript to the publisher, agreeing on cover art, making decisions on fonts, page size, and many other things. It also involved spending thousands of dollars to print, store, and ship books to Amazon and other retailers as orders were received. Today all I have to do is upload the finished book to Amazon's Kindle Direct Publishing to publish eBooks, making them available on Amazon's Kindle readers, through my website, and even print physical books on demand.

The 'i' moniker was blatantly appropriated from Apple's now famous 'i' product names. Steve Jobs originally used the 'i' to stand for internet, as the iMac came to market when the internet was first becoming pervasive. As the 'i' migrated to other products such as the iPod, it morphed in meaning towards individual, as Apple's products evolved into more personal devices like the iPhone.

The Age of 'i', as used here, refers to the increasing customization and personalization of digital experiences to the individual in front of the screen. This includes content, advertisements, recommendations, even graphical images, designed to increase engagement through relevancy to the particular individual. This personalization is quickly coming to the physical world as 3D printing expands from manufacturing to consumer goods and even food. And tools like augmented and virtual reality, again incorporating contextual relevancy to the individual user, begin to blur the line between the digital and physical experiences.

In short the world is increasingly becoming tailored to you as an individual.

This new world is antithetical to the massive consumer goods retail industry. This book explores the impact of the Age of 'i' on retail, including shopper expectations and the challenge traditional retailers face.

In this context, the 'i' most importantly stands for *individual,* as I have been convinced for nearly two decades that retail would return to a focus on the individual customer. This belief in the power of leveraging technology to return focus to the customer took seed as I learned the power of customer intelligence growing out of launching and operating one of the first loyalty programs in supermarket retail. It blossomed when my team and I created and implemented SmartShop, retail's first true personalized marketing solution over a decade ago. All my learning and all my experience across the industry have done nothing but reinforce the notion that aligning all activity to the individual customer is the industry's destiny.

Throughout this book the 'i' stands for other things as it pertains to this future vision of retail. *Immersive* is appropriate as the digital and physical worlds of commerce meld into a new shopping experience. *Intelligent* is equally appropriate as the ability to successfully market to, engage with, and provide products and services to the individual customer requires massive levels of intelligence about the person and the products. *Integrated* is a foregone conclusion; extensive and deep integration of systems and processes is required to even be on the playing field.

The last 'i', unsurprisingly, stands for *innovation*, inescapable given the increasing pace of change as technology fuels an ever-expanding universe of capabilities.

I am fortunate to have a unique position and experience with which to view the retail landscape of yesterday, today, and tomorrow. Years of retail experience, the opportunity to work with notable retailers and brand manufacturers around the world, and an unparalleled view to new innovation flowing into the retail industry permit me to not only observe and comment but to suggest key themes and direction to portend future success.

Any period of great change is accompanied by winners and losers. While I see significant challenges ahead for certain sectors of the massive retail industry, I also see unbridled opportunity for retailers of any size to leverage new cloud-based capabilities to transform their businesses and partner with their customers as we journey into the Age of 'i'.

We do indeed live in interesting times.

Chapter 1

Introduction: Reclaiming Retail's Customer Heritage

Today will be the slowest pace of change in your lifetime. Consider that for a moment. The ubiquitous iPhone was introduced just a decade ago, and today we take the app store and all the capabilities we have in our hand for granted. It seems like only yesterday that robots were the realm of science fiction, yet today we find them roaming store aisles, autonomous pods delivering groceries, and automated warehouses fast becoming the norm. Even the production of food itself is being transformed as meat is grown in factories and greens are grown in trailers alongside the store.

The fast moving consumer goods retail industry is in chaos and the shift online is only the tip of the iceberg as disruption sweeps across every part of the supply chain. And this disruption is only just getting started. Technologies are converging, triggering even greater growth in world-changing capabilities. And even industries are converging as new technologies, consumer interest, and economic forces come into play.

Many retailers are being whipsawed by the shift online and the explosive growth of innovation, not knowing where to focus next. Amidst this chaos, some retailers are trying to do everything while others are overwhelmed to the point of paralysis. And all retailers are moving too slowly, often not understanding the underlying forces at work driving this new world.

Five year plans, a staple of management, are obsolete before the save button is clicked as new capabilities, new competitors, and new consumer demands arise almost daily. To bring order to the chaos retailers need to focus on the one constant that is ever-present: *The customer*.

We have entered the Age of 'i'. This is a time of quickening innovation; expanding intelligence powered by artificial intelligence feeding off big data, and immersive experiences provided by augmented and virtual reality, with all of it increasingly focused on making the world all about each individual person.

Retail in the Age of 'i' reclaims the industry's heritage of customer focus growing from the days of the corner store. Today, retailers have the ability to leverage vast new technologies to once again focus on the individual customer, partnering with each customer as we journey forward.

And beyond technology, retailers have an opportunity to inject humanness into a shopping experience that is at risk of becoming an automated, people-free process of replenishment. The retail industry is rapidly approaching a crossroads. One path is leading to an efficient, cost-effective, yet sterile, shopping environment ruled by automation. The other is positioning technology in service to customers, taking advantage of automation to redirect human associates to engage with shoppers in either the physical or virtual environments, and fostering the personal relationships between the merchant and the customer that were a part of life decades ago.

"Throughout history, human beings have inherently been social creatures. For millions of years we've genetically evolved to survive and thrive through the "togetherness" of social groups and gatherings. Today, modern communication and technology has forever changed the landscape of our human interaction, and as such, we often decline without this type of meaningful personal contact. Today's highly individualistic, digitally remote, and material driven culture is now challenging all of this, as we turn to science to unlock the mysteries of human connection and wellness in a digitally connected world."[1]

I believe there is business opportunity in doing the right thing for people and our communities. That people today, staring into their digital screens for hours at a time, interacting via

Facebook or Twitter, and being drawn to every new shiny piece of tech, actually covet human connectedness. Retailers, especially food retailers, are in a unique position to deliver this powerful human experience given that people still need to eat daily and, as we'll see later in the book, the growing connectedness between food and health and wellbeing.

From a business perspective, every customer interaction, whether in the digital realm or the physical store, is vital to acquiring, growing, and retaining customers. Focusing on each individual customer forces retailers to think beyond generalizations - investing in a health and wellness program is good for my shoppers - to focus on leveraging technology to serve the individual; 'how can I help Sasha improve her life by providing products and services contextually relevant to her?'. This involves not looking at Sasha as representative of a cohort, but - literally - building a relationship with Sasha as an individual.

Not only is the customer the only constant in today's world of non-stop disruption, but customers are expecting, even demanding, that the world be made relevant to them. And why not? Consumers take for granted the personalization and relevancy in the digital world, and expect the same from brick & mortar retailers.

The New Realities of Scale

The good news: Thanks to the cloud and ever cheaper processing power, access to sophisticated technology has never been greater. Merriam Webster defines democratize as "*to make (something) available to all people.*" We are witnessing the democratization of technology as solution providers put increasingly powerful solutions in the cloud, making industry-leading capabilities available to retailers of all sizes.

This sea change in how technology is made available opens the door to significant opportunity for brick and mortar retailers. No longer does a retailer - or brand manufacturer - need to purchase costly computer hardware, pay for expensive software licenses, and bear the burden of expensive IT staff to manage it all. Instead, merchants can simply open the browser on their inexpensive tablet or smartphone and log-in.

Regional retailers have the opportunity to leapfrog their larger competitors, much as developing countries deploy the latest cellular communications technology, bypassing costly landline systems. While scale remains important, it is less so in the digital Age of 'i'. As always, retailers of any size must leverage their strategic assets to succeed, be they local community connections or massive innovation budgets.

Rather than size and scale, the defining factor dictating success today is a retail company's willingness to embrace change and innovation. When technologies quickly become widely available, it is the retailer's culture that becomes important, the willingness to embrace new capabilities, new ways of doing things, and seizing opportunities to truly partner with customers in creating the future of shopping.

But just like a populace gaining the right to control its destiny, there are responsibilities that accompany this transformation. Traditional retailers must understand there is a window of opportunity to leverage the technologies available to them to transform their businesses. Some of the executives I talk to across the country understand this, and they personally dedicate time to staying abreast of how the latest capabilities can benefit their business strategy. Some of these retailers are keen to pilot new solutions in an effort to learn, and others are aggressively bringing new solutions into the market to gain an edge over their competitors, new and old.

But other retailers - too many in my mind - hang back, looking to follow, or even worse, bury their head in the sand, refusing to acknowledge a rapidly changing retail world. Technology alone is not a silver bullet for the retail industry, but retailers and brands that ignore new capabilities are destined to become cannon fodder as increasing innovation transforms retail.

Retail in the Age of 'i' is about returning the customer to the nexus of the incredibly competitive and dynamic retail industry. With the individual customer once again ensconced, there are an additional four 'i's that retailers must focus on today in support of the individual shopper to achieve success tomorrow.

Powering the ability to engage with the individual customer is fast growing *intelligence*, big data from increasing sources to provide an unparalleled understanding of each shopper. There's a need to tightly and deeply *integrate* key systems to provide the seamless and cohesive *immersive* shopping experiences customers demand today. And, of course, there's a need to constantly *innovate* with a focus on growing the value of each individual customer.

If you're keeping score, I have identified five 'i's that will be crucial for retail going forward.

1. *Individual*
2. *Intelligence*
3. *Integration*
4. *Immersive*
5. *Innovation*

These five 'i's, in support of a focus on the individual customer, create a new construct for the retail industry. It's one made possible at scale only by technology, yet one that can foster the importance of human relationships.

We can define this new construct as:

> *iRetail* (def): **A new worldview for retail where all activities are aligned with creating, building, and keeping relationships with each individual customer, using lifetime value as a proxy for measuring the quality and effectiveness of those efforts.**

This book is filled with a wide variety of insights and concepts to help motivate companies toward change that really matters. What is important, especially for retailers reading this book, is to keep an open mind, to consider the possibilities. It's easy to quickly dismiss an idea that doesn't align to your worldview. But I challenge you to think about what you don't know you don't know. That the world today, powered by exploding innovation in every direction, is no longer the world we have known in the past. The Taking Action chapter near the end of the book presents a series of questions and next steps to help you move forward. Making progress on these steps will improve the chances of winning in the Age of 'i'.

Change has historically come slowly to the massive retail industry, with many companies instead choosing to be 'fast followers,' letting someone else take the risk in a notoriously thin margin business. It is human nature to be reactive to change, often needing some level of crisis to spike adrenalin and trigger action. We need look no further than the mad dash to online instigated by Amazon's acquisition of Whole Foods.

I would suggest that a crisis is upon the fast moving consumer goods retail industry. According to Statista, consumers' weekly grocery shopping trips have declined from 2.1 visits per week in 2006 to 1.6 in 2018, a decline of 25%. The massive grocery industry is in flux, moving online faster than expected, according to the latest research from FMI and Nielsen, which now project that $100 billion of industry sales will be executed online by 2022, not 2025 as projected just months before. But the shift online is only one move on a much larger chessboard. Companies like Amazon are focused on outright disruption and the very business model the $800 billion dollar grocery retail industry has been built on makes retailers vulnerable.

Buckle your seatbelts, we're in for a bumpy ride.

CHAPTER 2

Understanding the Age of 'i'

Look about and you see that the world is becoming increasingly tailored to you, your interests, and your needs. We have come to take for granted the personalization and relevancy in the digital world, no longer thinking about our customized news feeds. We give no thought to the complexity of systems and algorithms driving the process of sorting through nearly 600 million products sold by Amazon, or the thousands of movies available on Netflix. The work behind the scenes provides us with relevant recommendations. We simply see the suggestions put in front of us and, more often than not, make a purchase.

AI Drives Customization

The recent growth of artificial intelligence is powering yet more customization in the digital world. It is AI powering the voice-enabled digital assistants like Amazon's Alexa, Google's Assistant, and Apple's Siri. Amazon is intent on making Alexa ubiquitous in our lives, available not just in our homes but in our cars, offices, libraries, and even hospitals. The digital world is ours for the asking, any time, any place.

Forgot something for the dinner party tonight? Just ask Alexa to order it while you're driving to work. And Alexa is getting smarter. Amazon recently received a patent tied to Alexa's ability to recognize a user's physical and emotional states and respond to how you're feeling. Alexa can now tell if you're suffering from a cold and suggest ordering chicken soup from Whole Foods to be delivered in the next couple hours.

If you want to shop by voice, you're not limited to Amazon; Kroger recently joined Walmart, Walgreens, and other retailers providing consumers the ability to use Google Assistant to place online orders simply by speaking. Growing numbers of retail merchants are integrating to the predominant digital assistants, those provided by Amazon, Google, and Apple.

It is AI-powered voice recognition that is enabling a new world of services. Woebot is your virtual therapist available 24x7 through your smartphone. No need for a couch, no meds, and no dredging up childhood memories. Have a problem? Feeling sad or depressed? Just ask Woebot.

And if exercising is better than going to a therapist, Vi is at your service. Vi is your virtual personal trainer, accessing your workout data from your smartwatch, smartphone, and IoT-enabled equipment in the gym to provide realtime guidance — run faster! lift more! — communicated to you through your wireless headset.

Increasingly, the personalization found in the digital domain is manifesting in our physical world. 3D printing technology is helping drive this as shoes and clothing are created to our own individual specifications. Similar technology is being used to 'print' body parts and even organs. Nike's Configurator enables shoppers to customize their shoes, selecting colors and even materials. BareMinerals Made-2-Fit's app leverages the iPhone's camera and processing power to enable a user to scan their skin and get a custom makeup foundation delivered to their home with their name on the bottle, backed by a 100% Shade Match Guarantee.

And when the makeup is delivered to your home, you'll know it as you lie on the beach, receiving a notification on your phone. Opening the app, you can see and communicate with the driver through your smart doorbell. Voice-powered digital assistants connected to IoT devices enable you to customize your home to your desires simply by asking. While driving home you can ask Alexa to turn on the lights, warm the oven, and put some music on to greet you upon arrival. A growing number of smart appliances are connected to Amazon's automated replenishment service so you no longer have to be bothered to remember to reorder laundry detergent; your smart home can take care of that for you.

Kroger is working to make the brick and mortar store personalized to you. The company is deploying a new digital shelf display; one of its features will be lighting up relevant products for you as you walk down the aisle. Kroger is not only calling out relevant products as you shop but also personalizing the price to entice you to buy.

Online shoppers are increasingly able to tailor the delivery of products. You can have products delivered to your home, your office, the trunk of your car, available for pickup at the store on your way home, and more. You can reserve clothing online and find it waiting for you in the store's fitting room when you arrive. With Amazon's Key service you can even have the delivery person put your groceries in the refrigerator at home while you're at work. The world is increasingly your way.

Our very bodies are becoming the key to personalized services. Clear, the biometric airport security service, is now being used by Hertz to speed people through the car rental process. Customers that are Hertz members, and enrolled in the Clear service, can simply go to their car and exit through a special lane where either facial recognition or fingerprint biometrics are used to authenticate the person who can then go on their way.

Disney has used biometrics to verify ticket holders for some years now. Apple Pay, and similar services, use either finger scan or facial recognition to validate payment transactions. Some employees of Three Square Market, a Wisconsin-based tech company, have had microchips implanted in the subdermal layer of skin between their thumb and finger. The chips can be used to replace security badges, authorize payment transactions, and enable other conveniences.

And what is perhaps the ultimate in personalization, medicine and healthcare are rapidly becoming tailored to the individual, using the person's genome and other bio-markers. The use of technology to gather realtime health data from wearables, combined with a person's genomic blueprint, can help doctors assess an individual's disease susceptibility and develop personalized treatment plans.

This movement is already underway. The Isala Hospital in the Netherlands is using 3D food printing to customize meals to ensure that each person receives the nutrition needed to get them better faster.

Retailers Slow to Adapt

So we have a world increasingly customized to each individual, not only in the digital world, but increasingly in the physical world. And yet much of the retail industry goes to market and operates largely as it did fifty years ago with weekly ads filled with mass promotion, the same products, services, and prices for all.

At the core of this tumult is technology-fueled innovation. Retail executives are used to brick and mortar competitors of all types, from low cost, limited assortment stores like Aldi, Save-

A-Lot, and Family Dollar, to more highbrow operators like Wegmans and Whole Foods. What retail executives are not accustomed to is competing with some of the world's largest and most powerful technology companies and a plethora of nimble, young startups gunning to transform a lethargic industry. This is an entirely new playing field where disruption is the new normal.

Retail executives are poorly prepared for this new world, accustomed to a slow-moving industry and a time when retailers dictated industry change and innovation. Today, retail companies are adrift in a world of increasingly fast change across the supply chain as consumers rapidly adopt new technologies and new competitors spring forth at a bewildering pace.

Too many retailers are dealing with the symptoms of innovation rather than addressing the underlying forces. And this approach is dangerous, leading executives to make short-term tactical decisions without benefit of understanding the larger battle being waged.

Consumed with the nuts and bolts tactical execution required to simply stay alive in such an intense, high volume, low margin business, retail leaders are challenged to step back and understand the vast forces at work. And yet they must.

Welcome to the Age of 'i'.

CHAPTER 3

A New Worldview

I want to challenge the way you believe the world works. And then suggest to you a new perspective.

The place to start is understanding that our worldview is constrained by the knowledge available to us. We know what we know; for example, I know how to ride a bike. Then there are things that we know we don't know; I know that I don't know how to speak Russian. But then there are the things we don't know that we don't know.

The faster things change, the less reliable our predictions of the future are because the very things that can cause massive disruption may not even have been invented yet. We don't know what we don't know.

This is the dangerous place retail executives find themselves: Not knowing what they don't know. Not knowing what disruption lurks around the next corner. Retailers, like everyone, are working from a certain knowledge set that by default limits their understanding of what is possible. And yet to compete successfully, let alone survive, retail executives must throw some light on the vast abyss to bring some of what they don't know they don't know into the light. Said another way, retailers must adopt a new worldview.

Today, we as human beings are already in transition. We know the world is changing even if we don't know why.

Exponential Growth: Tomorrow Will No Longer Resemble Today

We are at the knee of the exponential growth curve of computer processing power and from this day forward change will be increasingly noticeable and increasingly fast. While most are familiar with the definition of exponential growth, far fewer people truly understand the power and implications of this reality. We as human beings are wired to think linearly. Today is much like yesterday and we have lived our lives expecting that tomorrow will be much like today. Except that is no longer true, and this will become increasingly apparent. Physicist Albert Bartlett is blunt in his assessment: "The greatest shortcoming of the human race is our inability to understand the exponential function."

Today is the slowest pace of change you will experience in your lifetime.

Let's use a story to illustrate the power of exponential growth.

Imagine you have a pond that is 4,000 square feet in size. There are fish in this pond and the fish need sunlight to live (the sunlight oxidizes the water through photosynthesis). There is a single lily pad on the surface that takes up exactly 1 square foot. Now imagine that every day, the number of lily pads double. (On day 2, there are 2 lily pads, on day 3, there are 4 lily pads, etc.)

Now, without doing the math in your head, guess how long will it take for the entire pond to be filled with lily pads and for all the fish to suffocate and die? 30 days? 60 days? Not even close. It would take less than 13 days for the entire pond to be filled with 4,000 lily pads. Let's go through each day:

Day 1: 1 lily pad
Day 2: 2 lily pads
Day 3: 4 lily pads
Day 4: 8 lily pads
Day 5: 16 lily pads
Day 6: 32 lily pads
Day 7: 64 lily pads

Let's stop there for a moment. On day 7, we are already more than half way toward all of the fish in our pond suffocating to death, and yet we only have 64 lily pads, meaning there is still 3,936 square feet of open pond water left; to put it another way, we still have 98.4 percent of our total resources left. Let's continue and see where the next 6 days take us.

Day 8: 128 lily pads
Day 9: 256 lily pads
Day 10: 512 lily pads
Day 11: 1024 lily pads
Day 12: 2048 lily pads
Day 13: 4096 lily pads

The day before all the fish died (Day 12), they still had plenty of sunlight. Almost half of the pond was still open to sunlight. In less than 24 hours they were all dead. Such is the threat of exponential growth. If you don't understand what it looks like, it can catch up to you and destroy you before you even understand what is happening. Here is a chart tracking the quick demise of these imaginary fish.[2]

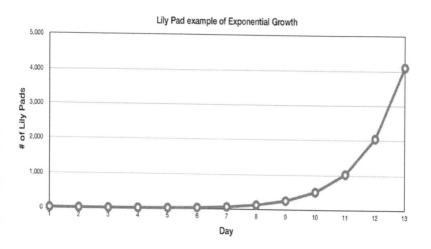

Now instead of lily pads, think about technology-fueled innovation.

Consider the implications of this. *The faster things change the less reliable our predictions of the future are because the very things that can cause massive disruption may not even have been invented yet. We don't know what we don't know.*

Historically, disruption would take long periods of time, often years, to be felt. Think about the shift from vinyl records to tapes to CDs to digital. That disruptive evolution played out over years. Now consider how much faster disruption is happening today. The Amazon Go store was opened to the public in January of 2018 and already we've seen a number of retailers moving to pilot similar technology provided by at least a half dozen young tech companies. This in addition to numerous retailers rolling out self-shopping apps as a way to provide cashier-less shopping. The pace of change is growing ever faster.

Am I beginning to change your view of how the world works today yet?

Let's look to another illustration to make this even more visceral.

Many readers will be familiar with Moore's law that states computer processing power doubles approximately every 18 months. Not as many may be familiar with Ray Kurzweil, noted author, technologist, and currently Director of Engineering at Google. Kurzweil uses the equivalent processing power of a $1,000 computer to convey the power of exponential growth. According to Kurzweil, in the year 2000 a $1,000 computer had the processing power equivalent to the brain of an insect. By 2015 that processing power had increased to the equivalent of the brain of a mouse. But here's where it gets interesting: By 2024 it is estimated that the $1,000 computer will have processing power equivalent to a human brain. And by 2045, less than 30 years from now, that same computer - comparable to the smartphone in your hand - will have processing power equivalent to the combined brains of every human being on the planet, an estimated 9 billion people.

The Power of Exponential Growth

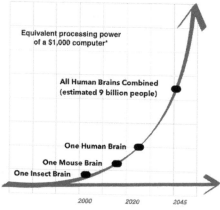

Equivalent processing power of a $1,000 computer*

All Human Brains Combined (estimated 9 billion people)

One Human Brain

One Mouse Brain

One Insect Brain

2000   2020   2045

In the year 2000, a $1,000 computer had processing power equivalent to the brain of an insect...

Fifteen years later, the $1,000 computer had the processing power equivalent to the brain of a mouse...

By 2022, that same $1,000 computer will have the processing power equivalent to a human brain...

And by 2045 that $1,000 computer will have processing power equivalent to the brains of all human beings combined

This is the new world we inhabit. And this world of exponential growth is one that retail industry executives must understand if they are to navigate the increasing turbulence ahead. The pace of change is no longer linear, it is exponential and this dictates a new worldview. *Tomorrow will no longer look like today.*

Consider the implications of ever-faster change. How do executives allocate resources; ensure they have associates with the requisite skill sets; develop and deploy training; develop, implement, and constantly update key processes, and far more. In my experience, a vast number of retail executives have failed to adequately consider the implications of exponential growth to their organizations and businesses.

IBM, at its Think 2018 conference, unveiled what it called the world's smallest computer, and it is *the size of a grain of salt*. The computer has processing power equivalent to an x86 chip circa 1990, but IBM is just getting started. IBM's vision is to embed these micro computers in products at the point of manufacture and packaging, connecting them to the cloud as IoT devices, and using the data to monitor products across the supply chain.[3]

It is this faster, cheaper processing power that is fueling the explosive growth of artificial intelligence and machine learning. It is AI powering self-driving vehicles. AI is powering digital assistants like Alexa and Siri. It is AI powering the next generation of optimization solutions. And it is AI powering the next generation of sophisticated hyper-personalized marketing capabilities.

Our intuition about the future is linear. But the reality of information technology is exponential, and that makes a profound difference. If I take 30 steps linearly, I get to 30. If I take 30 steps exponentially, I get to a billion.   *- Ray Kurzweil*

Amazon's Innovation Race

While technology capability is growing exponentially, the deployment of new capabilities in brick and mortar retail continues at a much more linear pace, giving rise to a growing innovation gap. And it is this gap that is particularly worrisome looking ahead.

To see evidence of this, we have to look no further than Amazon's 2018 Q3 results. Beyond the financial returns, Amazon announced 42 major product and service releases in that quarter alone. Things like a new family of Echo devices, new AWS services (including facial recognition in the cloud), and new Alexa capabilities (now offered on 20,000 different devices). The company announced the opening of the Amazon 4-Star store; the acquisition of PillPack, taking Amazon into the prescription drug business; grocery pickup from Whole Foods through Prime Now, and many other initiatives. Compare 42 major releases in *one quarter* vs. the number of major product or service announcements made by the typical brick and mortar retailer in a year. Therein lies the challenge for traditional retail.

The Growing Innovation Gap

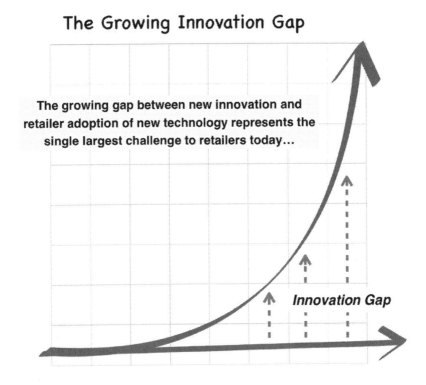

The growing gap between new innovation and retailer adoption of new technology represents the single largest challenge to retailers today...

Innovation Gap

"Companies are iterating not in years but in days," Groom (Kroger Technology's General Manager) said. "We're in a digital arms race. We're a 133-year-old grocery chain that's competing with companies that didn't exist a year ago."[4]

Jeff Bezos, Amazon's CEO, has long understood the value of being out in front as technology innovation fundamentally alters the rules of competition. While other companies have long based competitive strategy on technology, what's different is this point in time: We are at the inflection point on the exponential growth curve of computer processing power where noticeable change happens at an ever-increasing pace. Amazon is leveraging its innovation leadership position harnessed together with its vast resources to overwhelm the traditional retail industry, relegating many retailers to the proverbial corner convenience store.

We are at the inflection point on the exponential growth curve of computer processing power where noticeable change happens at an ever-increasing pace.

Sound familiar? It should. In the 1980s, then President Ronald Reagan, in what was to become known as the Reagan Doctrine, leveraged the powerful U.S. economy linked together with the country's burgeoning military innovation to launch an arms race with the Soviet Union. The result, as we all know, led to the collapse of the USSR and the end of the cold war.

Last year's acquisition of Whole Foods by Amazon triggered a grocery innovation arms race, throwing traditional retailers into a war few were prepared for. How bad is it? "Amazon spent nearly $23 billion on innovation research and development last year (2017), up 41% from the year before; more than any other U.S. company. That's more than Microsoft, Intel, Facebook and even Apple spent on R&D."[5] To put that in perspective for the grocery industry: A report from the IHL Group states that "Amazon's 2016 R&D spending was more than the top 20 retailers (excluding Walmart) technology spending combined... and about 75%-85% of (the top retailers) IT budgets is spent on simply maintaining and upgrading existing systems. As such, retailers are completely outgunned when it comes to spending on IT."[6]

What does Amazon have to show for that massive investment? Amazon holds 7,096 patents, receiving 1,963 patents in 2017 alone. By comparison, Walmart, the most prolific innovator among traditional retailers, holds just 349 patents.[7]

Here's more evidence of this 'Amazon doctrine' in action: The battle for voice-based commerce is already over. This, long before most retail executives know the battle had even started. "Purchases made through devices like Google Home and Amazon's Echo are projected to leap from $2 billion today to $40 billion by 2022."[8] Here's the kicker: "Amazon is forecast to have 70% of the voice-enabled speaker market this year (2018). By 2020, it's projected that there will be 128 million Alexa devices installed."[9] Amazon is aggressively expanding the Alexa platform, weaving it into everyday life, through partnerships with auto manufacturers, home appliance makers, and even Microsoft to bring Alexa into the workplace.

Transformation as the New Normal

This is not just about Amazon. Amazon's entry into new sectors like grocery and pharmacy has triggered a swarm of activity, creating a growing spiral of disruption. New capabilities, supplied by both young and old solution providers, add to the frenzy. The innovation arms race is not limited to a single battlefront; it has exploded across every part of the supply chain and there is no détente in sight.

Hardly a week goes by without some new transformative capability being announced and entering the massive retail industry. Walmart's Store No. 8 innovation lab is reported to review around 700-750 new solutions each year. The Center for Advancing Retail & Technology (CART) currently reviews an estimated 1,000 new capabilities flowing into the retail industry each year. How is a retailer to keep abreast of this? Let alone filter through the chaos of innovation to decide what to test, pilot, and deploy?

There are actually two sides to this innovation gap: A growing capability gap and a growing culture of innovation gap. And it is actually the latter that may be the most threatening to traditional merchants.

Forget about resources for a minute and consider what kind of company culture is capable of doing 42 major product and service releases in a three month period? Some of the largest retailers like Walmart or Kroger are expending vast resources on innovation but lagging far behind the digital behemoth.

Technology companies, especially younger startups, have very different cultures that thrive on finding reasons for how something can be done rather than the reasons why not. It is this openness to what is possible that avoids accepting the often self-imposed constraints and limits that business people seem to collect as they advance. And that innovation culture gap can be more limiting than actual resource constraints.

But we're just getting started.

Dr. Peter Diamandis is the Founder and Executive Chairman of the XPRIZE Foundation and the Executive Founder of Singularity University, a Silicone Valley institution that counsels the world's leaders on exponentially growing technologies. He gives us a view to what lies ahead and what he calls the Spatial Web or Web 3.0.

"The boundaries between digital and physical space are disappearing at a breakneck pace. What was once static and boring is becoming dynamic and magical.

Massive change is underway as a result of a series of converging technologies, from 5G global networks and ubiquitous artificial intelligence, to 30+ billion connected devices (known as the IoT), each of which will generate scores of real-world data every second, everywhere.

The current AI explosion will make everything smart, autonomous, and self-programming. Blockchain and cloud-enabled services will support a secure data layer, putting data back in the hands of users and allowing us to build complex rule-based infrastructure in tomorrow's virtual worlds.

And with the rise of online-merge-offline (OMO) environments, two-dimensional screens will no longer serve as our exclusive portal to the web. Instead, virtual and augmented reality eyewear will allow us to interface with a digitally-mapped world, richly layered with visual data.

Welcome to the Spatial Web."[10]

Diamandis goes on to suggest that these developments are already underway and that within the next two to five years the digital and physical worlds will increasingly merge, creating this spatial web. The notion of going online will disappear as each person will be continuously and seamlessly connected to an internet that envelops each of us and connects us to all the knowledge produced by humanity. We will be virtually accompanied by a cloud of data that knows our habits, behaviors, and preferences. Passwords as we think of them will disappear as biometric authentication provides automatic access to this new world.

And for all those readers thinking 'Sure, all this is possible but it's going to be a long time before it impacts me and my business,' remember: *Tomorrow is no longer going to look like today*.

CHAPTER 4

Retail in the Age of 'i'

My family's store started as a summer farmstand by my great-grandmother in 1934. I can remember as a kid getting up early on Saturday mornings to go to the regional market with my father, looking to buy fresh fruits and vegetables for sale that day, supplementing what we grew on our farm. My favorite part was swinging by a local bakery to pick up donuts and baked goods to sell. Nothing like a donut still warm from the fryer, just dripping with glaze.

What I also remember is how my grandfather seemed to know everyone. He knew Alice, and that she shopped on Wednesdays and loved fresh, local strawberries still warm from the field. He knew Ben, and that he liked his strip steaks cut extra thick. And even Mrs. Johnson and her dog Buck, a massive great dane, who loved getting a bone as a special treat from our meat department. I remember we shopped for Mrs. Gardner, delivering her groceries on our way home. And this was years before home delivery was a thing!

That was personalized retail. The customer was the most important part of the business.

And that was the constant refrain over the ensuing years. 'The customer is the most important part of our business' is the pablum I, and many others in the industry, was raised on.

Except something happened between then and now. Stores became bigger and busier. Product assortment exploded. Competition developed from every quarter. And food became available anywhere and everywhere.

As the industry grew larger we began to lose focus on the customer. How we made money - or at least how we thought we made money - began to shift. Merchandising — deciding what products to put on the shelves and which products to promote —became an exalted position in our organizations.

The increasing focus on products grew hand in hand with a growing focus on obtaining marketing funds from brand manufacturers. One could easily make the case that it was because of marketing funds that products grew to take center stage. Today, many major retailers would not be profitable were it not for those subsidies that support sale prices to the shopper, help offset advertising costs, bolster category margins, and enrich the bottom line.

In a very real sense, brand marketing funds have insidiously shifted retailer focus away from the customer to a dependency on products. Retail became product-driven.

But let's step back for a moment from retail to examine what's happening in the world around us.

As we saw earlier, 3D printing and augmented and virtual reality are transforming the world of mass produced goods. This signals a move from the industrial revolution to a world of customized products and services. The birth of the internet and the world wide web set the stage for the digitization of commerce, removing the personalization penalty for marketers who had to pay a high price for marketing differentiation in the physical world. In short, technology has fundamentally changed the world of one (product or service) to many (consumers) to a world of many (customized, personalized products or services) to one (shopper).

Beyond the world wide web, perhaps no technology has fostered consumer expectation of relevancy more than the smartphone. Mobile has brought with it a fast-growing expectation of contextual relevancy, the shopper knowing that merchants have access to technologies providing realtime location in a store or mall. Between the mobile browser and the countless apps available today, each of us has access to the world from the device in our hand, and increasingly that world is tailored to each of us individually.

And that brings us back to retail.

In the midst of this Age of 'i', the retail industry remains largely on the sidelines. Weekly ads, printed and distributed with the newspaper, filled with mass promotions, are simply out of sync with what our customers want today. Sure, some industry marketing vehicles have gone digital, but a digital version of the mass ad is spam and syndicated coupons are only relevant if I go searching for them.

But it doesn't have to be that way.

We as retailers can reclaim our customer heritage. We can use new technologies and capabilities to recreate those personal relationships of yesterday and become truly relevant to each of our individual customers today.

And that's what Retail in the Age of 'i' is all about. It is about fulfilling the destiny of retail by regaining a focus on the customer. It is about building relationships with each and every one of our individual customers. And it is about returning products to their rightful role in service to each of our customers.

The Question Retailers Should Be Asking

It's not easy for a generation of industry leadership that has come of age in the product-based world of mass retail to truly understand this shift, let alone accomplish it. Perhaps the way to get started is with a series of questions.

Today, retailers inevitably ask 'How can I sell more products?'. This is a natural question since sales are measured by products sold, and products sold equate to dollars, and that's how we keep score. Some retailers may even ask 'Who are my shoppers?', though this is really asked from a product perspective; more knowledge of my shoppers can help me sell more products.

Instead, turn the world inside out. And I mean really step outside who you are and let go of the way you see the world (through the eyes of a retailer). Put yourself inside the head of a shopper and ask:

'How can [enter the name of your retail store here] help me find, discover, and learn about the products I am interested in?'

Think for a moment how overwhelming it is to walk into a 60,000 square foot supermarket with 50,000+ products and find what you're looking for.

Now think about how retailers answer that question today:

'We'll send you a weekly ad with a few hundred products that are on sale, something in there should appeal to you.'

Or a response like this:

'We have 43,792 sku's of products on our shelves, so we have what you're looking for, you just have to find it.'

Let's try another quick exercise. Imagine Sasha is your customer. She's on the Whole 30 diet and her husband loves carbs and good Belgian beer. Her two year old loves protein and oranges and her six month old is just beginning to try some baby foods and Sasha really wants to buy organic.

So Sasha is walking into your store for the first time, or the 10th time, and asking *'How is [retailer] going to help me find, discover, and learn about the products I am interested in?'*.

How do you answer that? Sasha has two young kids with her, she doesn't have time to wander the aisles searching for a certain Belgian beer. She doesn't have time or patience to check each package label to see if it complies with the Whole 30 diet. You get the idea.

Consider this: Sasha can sit at home and, with a few mouse clicks, can find the products she's searching for on Whole Foods' website. The retailer just added more than a dozen filters for special diets and health concerns to their website, helping Sasha quickly find the products she wants, that can then be delivered or ready to be picked up.

Can your retail store help Sasha find what she wants?

Retailers take for granted that shoppers, after one or two visits, know where things are. In truth, the shopper is on their own to navigate those tens of thousands of products to find what they want.

Now let's try this. Put yourself in shopping mode again and open up Amazon's website and ask: *'How can Amazon help me find, discover, and learn about the products I am interested in?'*

Could Amazon answer the same way traditional retailers have answered that question for decades? Effectively saying to the shopper 'You're on your own'? No way.

Amazon unleashes its AI and machine learning recommendation engines on the shopper's user experience, serving up recommendations for products it thinks the shopper may be interested in from a previous visit or their browsing history.

Here's a way to think about it: Amazon takes a proactive approach to answering the shopper's question. Traditional retailers take a passive approach, assuming the customer will walk the store and page through the ad until they find what they're looking for. But assuming that past approach will continue to work when there are new competitors like Amazon is dangerous.

Hopefully that exercise of asking questions has opened up the possibility of a new way to think about retail for you. And if it did, great. But we're not done.

Now think about the thousands, hundreds of thousands, or millions of individual customers you have, each one of them asking themselves that question. *'How can [retailer] help me find, discover, and learn about the products I am interested in?'*

Retailers in the Age of 'i' must find a way to answer that question *for each and every one of their customers*, knowing that each customer's circumstances are unique. Think about the possible combinations of food tastes and preferences, the myriad health concerns, food allergies, budget constraints, pets, and on and on and on.

Until recently this would be an exercise in futility. But no longer. Technology provides the tools to answer that question for each and every individual customer. Retailers just need to think differently.

Retailers are Vulnerable

You hear every day about the transformation and disruption going on across the massive retail industry. Much of it about the shift online, with some studies projecting 20% or more of grocery sales will move online in just the next few years. While online grocery shopping has been around for over fifteen years, it was Amazon's acquisition of Whole Foods that lit the fuse, triggering a mad rush to online that is consuming the industry.

But I want to suggest something else to you. The move online is simply the opening move on a much larger chessboard. Companies like Amazon are playing a longer game, looking beyond just shifting some portion of retail sales to online, instead focused on completely upending the massive grocery retail industry.

And nearly every retailer is vulnerable.

Putting the individual customer at the center of a retailer's activities includes developing marketing relevant to the shopper. The power of marketing personalization has been well documented. We have to look no further than the success Kroger has had over the past 15 years. Other retailers like Albertsons-Safeway and Ahold are following suit. Retailers doing an even moderately good job with marketing personalization report participating customer spending up 5% or more. When I was still a practicing retailer, we saw year-on-year increases of 7% or more.

And yet for all that impact, marketing personalization hasn't really taken hold. It remains an incremental initiative, layered on as an afterthought. Why is that?

Marketing personalization has not spread for two reasons. The first is because retailers inevitably want someone else to pay for it, that someone else being the brands. The second is that retailers don't believe shoppers truly value it. Executives often think, "If marketing personalization is valuable to my shoppers, why aren't more of them opening my emails?"

Let's take the latter first. Why is marketing personalization as executed by most retailers today not perceived as truly valuable to the shopper? That's because it's typically delivering only minimal value. When thinking marketing personalization, many retailers think in terms of taking the couple hundred products in the weekly ad, or maybe even the couple thousand TPR (temporary price reduction) deals across the store, and filtering that mass content to communicate, say, the ten most relevant promotions to the shopper.

While aiding shopping convenience, this approach does not create any added economic value for the shopper. Its not like the retailer is extending a special deal just for the specific shopper; instead the retailer is just helping the shopper navigate to the mass promotion. Is it any wonder that shoppers have a tepid response to this approach?

Retail in the Age of 'i' portends a complete upending of the traditional, product-driven, marketing funds-dependent, retail business model.

More pertinent to why marketing personalization has not grown is that retailers inevitably are looking for someone - the brand manufacturer - to fund any added savings and even the cost of targeting and communicating the deal to the shopper.

Now stop to think about that for a moment. If brands are being asked to fund additional offers, they are going to demand a return on that spend and often want some say as to where their money is going, which may or may not ultimately align with the retailer's goals. While the retailer wants to give Alice a savings on her favorite brand of whipped cream to go with her fresh strawberries, the brand may view that as a waste, assuming they will already get Alice's purchase, and instead want to target buyers of competing brands.

And therein lies the challenge for traditional retailers in the Age of 'i'. A dependency on brand marketing funds is directly counter to fostering, and growing, a relationship with each individual customer, accomplished, in part, by providing meaningful savings on products the customer wants to buy.

Retail in the Age of 'i' portends a complete upending of the traditional, product-driven, marketing funds-dependent, retail business model. The technology is available today to understand what specific products will appeal to each individual customer in any given week. The technology is available to not only understand what products to promote to each individual customer, but also what discounts, if any, need to be provided to each shopper to get them into the store (either physical or digital store), grow their basket, and increase retention over time.

Shoppers, smartphone in hand, are waiting for retailers to provide them relevant savings on the products they want to buy. Retailers wondering how to increase digital engagement need wonder no longer. Relevant savings is a powerful proposition to encourage customers to engage across digital channels, be it via a retailer's website, email, app, or text, to learn about their personalized promotions. This is Retail in the Age of 'i'.

Many readers will be shaking their heads, thinking to themselves 'here we go again, someone thinking that the massive retail industry is going to be upended because of some newfangled idea'.

This time is different. Remember where we are on the exponential growth curve of technology. Look around to see the virtual and physical world being tailored to each individual's needs, wants, and desires. Is retail immune from this trend? *Tomorrow is no longer going to look like today*.

Here's the scary part: What happens when Amazon starts going to market applying its vast expertise in AI and machine learning to the trove of customer data it is collecting from

Whole Foods customers identifying themselves at checkout via their Prime membership?

Whole Foods doesn't sell big CPG brands, instead focusing on a strong private label line, natural and organic products from smaller producers, and considerable sales of fresh foods. Whole Foods is not chained to brand manufacturers for profitability. Instead, Amazon is free to unleash its powerful recommendation technologies on the entire Whole Foods product assortment, giving each individual shopper savings on specific products relevant to them individually.

Unbeholden to brand manufacturers, Amazon is free to give Alice savings on her favorite brand of whipped cream. Free to give savings to Ben on the steaks he likes. And free to provide personalized savings to each and every Whole Foods shopper. Amazon is positioned to quietly grow share of wallet, attracting more and more business from shoppers as it builds and deepens relationships, those gains increasingly coming from its traditional competitors.

And if that's not enough, Amazon has recently announced a nationwide expansion of Whole Foods, including bringing two hour Prime Now delivery to all stores.

Think this can't happen? Ask some of the retailers that have lost sales to, or even been driven out of business by Kroger's marketing personalization. Many traditional retailers still do not yet realize the power of marketing personalization, stealth marketing at its finest. You, as a competing retailer, simply do not and cannot know what promotions are being communicated to shoppers in your marketplace.

What happens when Amazon unleashes its vast expertise in AI and machine learning on the trove of customer data it is collecting from customers identifying themselves at checkout via their Prime membership?

I can remember talking with Michael Moore (not the filmmaker), who at the time was the Chief Marketing and Ecommerce Officer for Lowe's Foods in North Carolina, about Kroger's acquisition of Harris Teeter in 2013. In the time subsequent to the takeover, Michael related to me that Harris Teeter became very aggressive with weekly promotions across the market, driving hard to reverse a perception that Harris Teeter had become high priced.

The aggressive promotions lasted for a period of several months and then everything went quiet. What happened was that Kroger invested in improving Harris Teeter's price perception in the market and growing store traffic. That accomplished, Kroger then segued tactics, leveraging the company's famed marketing personalization to take over driving sales and margins. Kroger executed a classic 'shock and awe' campaign to improve Harris Teeter's price perception and then sent in Seal Team 6 in the form of stealth marketing personalization to continue the battle.

Back to Amazon's Whole Foods. By now some readers will begin to understand the power of marketing and pricing personalization to quietly grow share of market to the detriment of competing retailers. Other readers, not yet convinced of their vulnerability, will be thinking 'OK, but Whole Foods is still catering to a small demographic of shoppers with their product assortment so I don't have to worry too much'. Fair enough. But consider this: Younger shoppers — and I would suggest shoppers of all ages — are paying much more attention to the foods they are consuming, increasingly avoiding big-brand packaged foods. The Whole Foods assortment, when relevant products are marketed at meaningful prices to each individual customer, now looks like a different threat entirely.

The traditional supermarket industry is vulnerable to disruption because of its dependency on brand manufacturer marketing funds. That very dependency is diametrically opposed to a world where a retailer goes to market promoting whatever product is meaningful to each individual customer.

Now many readers may take exception to this for a multitude of reasons. But my point is this: Whether it is Amazon's Whole Foods or some other retailer - maybe an established retailer who decides to disrupt themselves by upending the legacy product-driven model, or even a new upstart - Retail in the Age of 'i' is going to happen. The only discussion is how fast and by whom.

It is this conundrum, a product-driven dogma vs. a customer-focused creed, that lies at the heart of retail industry disruption. I would suggest that the very business model of grocery retail, product-driven merchandising fueled by manufacturer marketing funds, is the straw that will break the proverbial camel's back in the time ahead. In the Age of 'i' everything is about the individual customer, not about what brand or product is going to provide inside margin.

Let me say this a different way: **The traditional fast moving consumer goods retail model, dependent upon manufacturer marketing monies to fund discounts, category margins, and the bottom line, is antithetical to the Age of i philosophy and** *is the very thing that makes FMCG retail ripe for disruption.*

And that should keep you awake at night.

Just how vulnerable is the grocery retail industry to the disruption I'm suggesting? Very. Only 23 out of the top 50 supermarket retailers [11] have comprehensive customer identified purchase data. Most - not even all - of the others rely upon eCommerce (customer identified by default) or digital coupons (customer must create a digital wallet) to identify what is a small portion of total transactions to customers. The traditional grocery industry is woefully unprepared for Retail in the Age of *i*.

Not Just Transformation; Complete and Utter Disruption

Disruption occurs when an established business model is upended, not just changed. Sometimes this occurs by an upstart taking a different view of a business, irrespective of technology. Costco's subscription model disrupted the traditional retail model by selling goods at a price to cover operating costs and using annual membership fees to power bottom line profitability. Other times technology is an enabler, for example helping Netflix upend the once all-powerful Blockbuster. Or Apple's iTunes and iPods disrupting the music industry. It is not technology capability itself that causes the disruption, it is the ability to do things differently because of technology that upends staid business models.

I believe outright industry disruption is the long-game Amazon is playing. Amazon is positioning itself to take advantage of the industry's dependence on brand marketing funds as retail shifts to the Age of 'i'. The development of grocery to online is but one move, albeit a big one, on the larger chessboard. There is speculation by some industry pundits that Amazon has peaked, pointing to the slower growth of grocery when compared to Walmart's online initiative. But I believe Amazon is just getting started. Much of Amazon's activity at Whole Foods to date has been focused behind the scenes, making distribution more efficient, preparing for significant growth of private label products, and more.

The long-awaited move to link Prime membership with Whole Foods shopping is now in place, helping Amazon build a vast repository of customer-identified food purchases. The shopper's Prime identification is making it easy for Amazon to link food purchases with all other purchases made on Amazon's massive platform. And, as we'll see in an upcoming chapter, Amazon's coming ability to link food purchases to prescription drug purchases, will connect all the dots as food and health converge.

I believe outright industry disruption is the long-game Amazon is playing. Amazon is positioning itself to take advantage of the industry's dependence on brand marketing funds as retail shifts to the Age of 'i'.

The move to selling groceries online does not upend the traditional, product-driven business model and its dependency on brand marketing funds. Yes it certainly changes it. But the shift online in and of itself is not as much disruptive as it is transformative.

Merriam-Webster defines disruption as to break apart, to rupture. That is what Retail in the Age of 'i' is about; a complete disruption of the old model, moving from mass marketing to true individualized marketing. But it goes even further. Not only are marketing and pricing made relevant to each individual customer, but the very product assortment, both in-store and online, becomes increasingly relevant to the individual. Food is becoming customized to the individual. Remember the Isala Hospital using 3D printing to tailor each meal to the individual patient? *Tomorrow will no longer resemble today.*

That is what Retail in the Age of 'i' is about: A complete disruption of the traditional business model, moving from mass marketing to true individualized marketing.

Change is Hard

Clayton Christensen, author of the Innovator's Dilemma, has clearly identified the difficulty of creating disruptive innovation within an existing business. Owners and investors wish to protect the profitability of the status quo. Management, associates, and even customers like the safety and security of a world they know. And yet the typical retail strategy of being a 'fast follower' is a recipe for disaster in today's increasingly fast paced world. Retail in the Age of 'i' rewards speed and boldness, and punishes the slowness and safety of yesterday's approach.

> *"To put it another way: When faced with a competitor like Amazon, do you do as Walmart did, and invest heavily in tech firms and technical knowledge? Or do you go the way of Sears...into bankruptcy court?"[12]*

In the 2004-2007 period, Pay by Touch was the country's hottest startup, attracting an estimated $400 million in funding from large hedge funds and private equity groups. Like moths to a flame, investors were drawn to the company's intellectual property and innovative technology that enabled a shopper to access a digital wallet biometrically at checkout. A simple finger scan and a PIN number would trigger payment and more.

Separately, in 2003 my team and I had started building SmartShop, the first true personalized marketing solution for mass retail, and subsequently sold the technology and IP to Pay by Touch in late 2005. The proposition was simple: shoppers could obtain their personalized deals at a kiosk in the store (along with web and email) and then receive the personalized savings at checkout simply by scanning their finger. To the amazement of McKinsey Consulting, Accenture, and others - all of whom were involved in the innovative startup - we engaged more than half the customer households shopping each week, touching more than 65% of total sales.

Though Pay by Touch ultimately failed for other reasons (another story for another day!), I share this anecdote to provide context for a fascinating meeting in 2006 with Catalina

Marketing. Catalina, as many know, is the company that prints the coupon offers at checkout triggered by your brand purchases. Catalina at the time had recently been acquired by a private equity group and some saw the synergy that could be created in pairing Catalina's large sales force, access to CPG brand budgets, and retail deployments with PBT's marketing personalization capability. While there was much apparent synergy, at the end of the day Catalina could not disrupt its own successful business model away from being brand-driven to customer-focused.

Formerly a cash-printing machine, Catalina was disrupted right into Chapter 11, filing for bankruptcy in December 2018.

The Staid Supermarket Industry is Ripe for Disruption

Dave Dillon, the past CEO of Kroger, is credited with leading the development of the company's Customer First strategy, which has been fundamental to Kroger's success over the past fifteen years. "The strategy called for the company to make the customers' interests foremost in every decision it makes. It included lowering prices, targeting ads and improving store locations to serve customers better."[13]

As the strategy powered Kroger to success over the past decade, the approach has slowly spread across the industry, where it has become known as customer centricity. And customer centricity, at its core, is based upon leveraging customer data-driven insights and analytics to inform product assortment decisions, assist in promotion planning, pricing decisions, and, of course, marketing personalization.

Fifteen years after Kroger rolled out its strategy, many multi-billion dollar regional retailers have decided to embark on a similar path, leveraging data and process changes to supposedly put the customer at the center of their marketing and merchandising activity. As these retailers look to graft a customer focus onto their traditional product-centric merchandising activity, they often turn to expensive legacy solution providers to assist, companies like Dunnhumby, Symphony AI Retail, Precima, Aimia, and others.

The approach used by these companies is to leverage data and insights into accessing additional, hopefully incremental, marketing funds from the brands; these funds are intended to help the retailer defer the costs of the solutions and to help fund personalized offers. And while the goal may be worthy, I submit that at the end of the day a retailer cannot serve two masters. How can a retailer be truly customer-focused if they are driven to maximize CPG brand marketing funds? That's an oxymoron of the first degree.

Certainly retailers cannot just walk away from the massive subsidy that brand marketing funds represent, and some retailers will argue that, understanding the conundrum, they can take measures to ensure that customer relevancy wins out over brand dollars. Except that it doesn't happen, not when category managers and merchandising executives are incentivized to maximize product sales and product margins.

How can a retailer be truly focused if they are driven to maximize CPG brand marketing funds? That's an oxymoron of the first degree.

A Shell Game

A related practice that goes hand-in-hand with 'customer centricity' initiatives is selling de-identified transaction data to major brands. Some regional retailers today participate in a loose consortium orchestrated by one of the solution providers to do just that, sell aggregated data from several regional retailers that, combined, generate enough sales volume to be of interest to big brand manufacturers. And where do the revenues gained from this effort go? In good part those funds go to pay the solution provider for their efforts, with the remaining balance split across the participating retailers... where it helps offset solution costs or helps bolster the bottom line. There is nary a customer in sight.

Having spent many years as a retailer, and many working with major retailers, CPG brands, and wholesalers about the world, I clearly get the attraction of this kind of approach. Leverage my data, combined with other similar retailers, to generate an incremental revenue stream from the brands and use those funds to help offset the cost of customer centric solutions that provide customer segmentation that can be used to improve merchandising. If only it were that easy.

Grocery retailers have played a shell game with brand marketing funds for decades. I can remember when Walmart entered the grocery business in the mid 1990s, shocking traditional retailers with their low prices. Retailer after retailer bemoaned to the brands or to their wholesalers that Walmart was selling products for less than the retailer was paying for them. And inevitably the traditional retailer was negotiating hard to get the lowest cost of product while having their other hand out looking for additional funds in the form of ad placement fees, in-store displays, slotting fees, and more.

Walmart, on the other hand, eschewed this practice, pushing vendors to put all marketing funds and any other monies into lowering the everyday cost of the product. Rather than playing the high-low game of traditional retailers, Walmart instead pushed an everyday low price, and went on to become the world's largest company by revenue.

Many Retailers are on the Wrong Path

It is fascinating to observe that while many regional retailers are pursuing this kind of customer-centric strategy, ultimately driven by CPG dollars, Kroger is moving to reduce it's dependency on brand marketing funds by growing the company's private label program. "In 2017, the retailer reached $20.9 billion in private label program sales, and reached $2 billion in annual Simple Truth sales, which McMullen (CEO) said is "remarkable considering the brand is only five years old." In a March 2018 investor call, "McMullen said that for the fourth quarter, private label made up 29.5% of unit sales and 26% of sales dollars, excluding fuel and pharmacy."[14]

Kroger is reducing its dependency on big CPG brands while many regional retailers are on the path of actually growing their dependence on brand marketing funds, and increasing their vulnerability to the coming disruption.

Private label product is important to retailers not only because of unique products exclusively available from the retailer, but also from the expanded gross margin provided. Consider what Kroger is doing: By expanding its private label sales, Kroger is reducing its dependency on big CPG brands, and positioning itself to use the expanded gross margin provided by private label to help fund more marketing personalization, providing the right product at the right price to each customer household with a goal of acquiring, growing, and retaining shoppers. Meanwhile, many competing regional retailers are on the path of actually growing their dependence on brand marketing funds, and increasing their vulnerability to the coming disruption.

And let's not forget about Amazon when thinking about private label. Leveraging its 100 million Prime member audience, Amazon has focused on the 68% of Americans who have pets. In mid-2018 Amazon launched Wag, its own private label line of dog food, apparently the beginning of a major expansion of the company's pet business.

But that's not all. The Cadent Consulting Group predicts that "Amazon, including its Whole Foods 365 Everyday Value brand, with an estimated $2 billion in sales added to Amazon's $2 billion grocery private label sales in 2017, will grow to $20 billion by 2027."[15]

Some may remember reports of a meeting Amazon held in May 2017 for large CPG brand manufacturers. The focus of the meeting was effectively to encourage the brands to sell direct through Amazon's platform. A subtle, though key part of the proceedings was Amazon encouraging brand manufacturers to redesign product packaging to be more eCommerce friendly. While the package of cookies with see through packaging looks nice on the shelf it does not hold up well when put in a box with other products and shipped direct to a consumer.

Retailers in the Age of 'i' reliant on brand marketing funds are entering the fight with both hands tied behind their back.

In an article I authored in June 2017, *Amazon's One-Two Punch*, I speculated that Amazon would follow its own prescription with regards to Whole Foods private label products, and indeed the company has done just that. "Sales through Amazon.com of the 365 Everyday Value brand from Whole Foods Market, which Amazon acquired at the end of August (2017), totaled $10 million in just three months."[16] Mind you, this was in a three-month period shortly after Amazon acquired Whole Foods. Imagine what's ahead.

Strong private label programs, with their expanded gross margins, are tailor-made for Retail in the Age of 'i'.

The focus here on private label is not so much a testament to the power of a private label strategy as it is on showcasing how key retailers like Kroger and Amazon are transitioning away from a dependency on CPG marketing funds, better positioning themselves for Retail in the Age of 'i' when success is dictated by a true customer focus, not brand-driven sales and a dependency on manufacturer marketing funds.

So Retail in the Age of 'i' is all about returning the customer to center stage, regaining humanity in retail through building relationships with each of our individual customers, and partnering with them as we move into the future.

But how do retailers do this, particularly larger retailers? Supporting the foundational focus on the first 'i', the individual customer, are four additional 'i's that are required to succeed. In the next chapters, we'll take a deeper look into all five 'i's that are required to navigate retail in the Age of 'i'. The individual customer is the first 'i', the common thread woven through these additional 'i's, uniting them into a cohesive strategy.

As a refresher, the other 'i's are:

- The need to leverage *intelligence* gleaned from big data to power customer relationships built around making every interaction relevant to the individual shopper.
- The importance of highly *integrated* systems and platforms to provide a seamless, comprehensive experience.
- The imperative of leveraging that knowledge and capability into providing *immersive* shopping experiences both online and in the store.
- The requirement to continuously *innovate*, discover, pilot, and deploy new capabilities. This will fulfill on the purpose of acquiring, growing, and retaining customers through an individualized focus.

We can collectively think of this approach as iRetail, a construct or new worldview for retailers moving forward. It is how well a retailer focuses on, implements, and executes against each of the 'i's that will dictate success in the time ahead.

CHAPTER 5

The Age of the Individual Customer

So the notion of growing your relationship with each individual customer sounds like a noble goal but how do you really operationalize something like this? Especially if you're a larger retailer with millions or even tens of millions of customers?

This is where new technologies become an ally rather than a foe. Retailers today have a unique opportunity to truly partner with each individual customer, bringing them along on the journey into the Age of 'i', deepening loyalty and relationships on the path to growing lifetime value. Think of it as enveloping each individual customer in their own personal ecosystem, fed by personalized and contextually relevant content fueled by everything known about the shopper while providing tools to customize services and experiences to his or her own liking.

Create a personal ecosystem for each individual customer giving them the power to customize their shopping experience, attuning marketing and even product discovery to their unique needs and wants.

Shoppers of Foodtown, the grocery retailer in the metro New York and northern New Jersey market, receive two emails each week relevant to the individual customer. The first is a personalized weekly ad; Foodtown filters the hundreds of items on sale to each individual customer, presenting the eight most relevant sale products for that customer that week. In similar fashion, Foodtown filters the hundreds of digital coupons available each week to present the six most relevant to each shopper. Foodtown is pushing to the shopper content that it knows is highly relevant to them individually at that point in time, using all the intelligence it gleans from historical purchase data.

Albertsons-owned Safeway has evolved it's Just for U program beyond relevancy like Foodtown's to provide personalized promotional pricing. As a shopper at Pavilions (a Safeway banner) in Southern California, where we live, we receive a weekly email with our exclusive deals, special pricing on relevant products.

Partner with your individual customers and bring them along with you on the journey into the Age of 'i'.

Kroger's Opt-UP health & wellness app provides the tools a shopper can use to tailor the shopping and product discovery experience to his or her own needs and preferences. In the Opt-UP app, a customer can easily filter the tens of thousands of products available in the typical Kroger store to discover those that have the highest general nutrition scores or those that are compatible with (for example) the Keto diet.

For Foodtown, Safeway, and Kroger it is technology that is powering the 'bubble' or ecosystem that each retailer is working to create around their individual customers. Increasingly, it is AI-powered capabilities delivered from the cloud that enable even mid-size retailers like Foodtown to provide sophisticated, personalized marketing to each of their customers.

Some Retailers are Trying

Retailers like Foodtown and Albertsons-Safeway are trying to focus on their shoppers through efforts like those described. But starting from a product-centric base makes the journey to iRetail an arduous one.

If we look back across fast moving consumer goods retail over the past 25 years, we can see a slow movement towards the shopper as the industry has evolved, seeking revenue and margin growth along with simple relevancy, as the world progresses.

The birth of early retailer frequent shopper programs was the first real step towards understanding shoppers in the modern world of mass retail, some of those early practitioners notching wins by recognizing and rewarding their regular customers. As bigger retailers began capturing customer data it quickly gained the attention of major consumer packaged goods brand manufacturers. For the first time, retailers had valuable data that was beyond the reach of the brand.

As larger retailers like Kroger increasingly pressured brand manufacturers to fund incremental promotional programs targeting offers to specific shopper audiences, brands quickly saw the improved ROI that promotion targeting delivered. And beyond direct increases in marketing effectiveness, the insights customer data were able to provide laid the foundation for the next step in the journey towards the customer: Shopper Marketing.

Shopper Marketing: No Longer Enough

Sometime around 2001 I was attending a retail conference on loyalty marketing when a speaker from Procter & Gamble put a slide up on the screen, referencing 'some grocer in upstate New York that's got this figured out'. What he had on the screen were the well-known opposing pyramids that I used to convey the idea that a retailer's handful of most valuable customers receive a disproportionately small share of a retailer's - and brand's - discounts and marketing investment.

That chance encounter led to work with Procter & Gamble, Unilever, and other major brands over the ensuing years. Beyond helping educate the brands about retail loyalty programs, much of our focus was leveraging customer-identified transaction data to devise collaborative marketing initiatives benefiting the brand and retailer, laying the foundation for the Shopper Marketing movement that continues to hold sway across the industry.

Shopper Marketing magazine defines shopper marketing as "A cross-functional discipline designed to improve business performance by using actionable insights to connect with shoppers and influence behavior anywhere along the path to purchase."[17]

Part of the challenge today is that the shopper path to purchase is no longer linear, or even sequential. A growing number of digital channels combined with the ability to be online anywhere has broken down preconceived notions of a shopper journey as a shopper can move from no intent to a purchase with the click of a button.

Shopper marketing has grown over the past decade to a commanding presence in the consumer packaged goods industry. Brand marketers today spend an estimated $50-60 billion annually on shopper marketing initiatives that continue to grow while traditional trade promotion budgets decline. Large brand manufacturers have built out massive shopper marketing departments within their organizations, employ legions of data analysts searching for insights and fund countless agencies conducting never-ending research.

Shopper marketing has established itself as a vital discipline in the retail industry.

But it's not enough.

Customer Centricity in the Age of 'i': A Modular Approach

Kroger's early efforts encouraging brands to fund incremental promotions targeted to grow customer spending coalesced into what we now think of as Shopper Marketing. But Kroger's strategy involved more than just targeted offers, and has helped give rise to the next step on the path back to a true shopper focus: Customer centricity.

Customer-centric retail strategy effectively focuses in on four key areas. These use customer data driven insights and analytics to make improved, supposedly customer centric, decisions in:

- **Product assortment:** Leveraging customer segments to help rationalize the product assortment at a group of similar stores or even the individual store.
- **Promotion planning:** Again using customer segments, working to ensure that the mass promotions each week serve to attract the desired shoppers.
- **Pricing:** Understanding key items by category that must be priced right based on shoppers.

- **Marketing personalization:** Using precision targeted offers to grow customer sales and improve customer retention over time.

In Kroger's case, the company relied on its early joint venture with Dunnhumby to power up this customer-centric strategy. Dunnhumby had come to fame helping Tesco, the UK's largest supermarket retailer, understand and use the customer data gathered through its loyalty program. In similar fashion, Dunnhumby's consulting & analytics approach, using hundreds of data analysts, helped power Kroger's success over many years. The effort became so core to Kroger's strategy that it acquired Dunnhumby USA's tech assets in 2015 and formed 48.51°, bringing the customer-focused initiative in-house.

As the customer-centric approach has spread, recently gaining momentum amongst mid-market regional companies, retailers have turned to what we can think of as legacy solution providers like Dunnhumby, Symphony Retail, Precima, Aimia, and others. Interestingly, many of these others were originally formed by alumnae of Dunnhumby, and so all have a similar approach. Effectively, each purports to be seen as a one-stop solution for retail customer centricity across the four key areas (assortment, promotion planning, pricing, and marketing personalization).

Essentially their approach is to segment a retailer's shopper base into meaningful cohorts, shoppers that are similar in behavior. Those segments are then used as filters at a store, region, ad group, banner, or company level to inform decision making in the areas called out above.

When it comes to marketing personalization, many more segments are created, driven by brand loyalty, discount propensity, and more, which are then used to iterate through to what specific promotion should be sent to the customer household. More recently, some solution providers have sought to bring newer technology to bear, making the targeting process more efficient and effective.

To a greater or lesser degree, these legacy solution providers approach the relationship with the retailer as a consulting or professional services engagement bundled with analytic and marketing services. And each of these solution providers ultimately relies on marketing funds from brand manufacturers to fund the efforts via the retailer.

Technology Provides A Better Way

Just as technology innovation is disrupting activity across the supply chain, so too is innovation impacting the legacy approach to customer centricity. New tools powered by AI and machine learning are obviating the need for massive teams of data analysts crunching through the vast storehouses of customer data. As is happening elsewhere, the business model of these legacy providers is being disrupted. New AI and machine learning capabilities are writing into software code what once required teams of analysts. Customer centricity is becoming a product.

But let me refine that. The cutting edge approach to customer centricity is now a modular approach as opposed to the one-stop legacy provider. And new capabilities, laser focused on each area, are being used to power up increased performance at far lower cost. If a retailer is going to rely on brand marketing funds, far better to spend as much of those funds as possible in delivering value to the shopper rather than millions of dollars in consulting and professional services fees paid to vendors.

Companies like Daisy Intelligence use AI and machine learning to help a retailer optimize mass promotions, understanding what promotion to run in a specific week and even at what price. The growing number of retailers using Daisy's capabilities are often realizing gains of 5 percent or more to revenue along with increases to gross margin by running the right promotion at the right time.

Other companies, like Pristine Infotech, leverage the latest technologies to help a retailer optimize product assortment and focus on strategic pricing of key items within each category most relevant to shoppers at a store level.

Marketing Personalization: Start With the Customer

Starting from a foundation of the mass marketing of products, loyalty, shopper marketing, and customer centricity have simply been way stations along the path to returning industry focus to the shopper.

Retail in the Age of 'i', however, is not the next consecutive step in the product-to-customer continuum. Rather, Retail in the Age of 'i' represents a complete upending of the industry's journey, beginning, not with products, but with the individual customer.

Step back for a moment and consider how you would create retail marketing if you were to start with a clean sheet of paper. Would you select a handful of products drawn from the 40,000+ sku's in the typical store to promote, knowing that only a few of those products and deal prices will be meaningful to a relatively small number shoppers across your market area? Or would you instead - and remember, we're starting with a clean slate - want to promote the specific products important to each individual customer at meaningful discounts and in sync with their purchase cycle?

Let's put this in the real world. A well known regional retailer had an estimated 707,000 customer households shop at least once in a recent three-month period. In any given week, only

149,000 customer households purchased one or more ad items. In other words, in any given week only 21% of customer households found any ad item to be relevant.

In the Age of 'i', retailers have vast intelligence and insight to each customer. Armed with this knowledge, retailers have the ability - for the first time - to move away from cyclic mass promotions and instead direct the right promotion and the right savings to the right customer at the right time and place. AI and machine learning have powered up strategic hyper-personalization and are forever changing retail marketing.

Forrester found that companies that fully invest in modern personalization will outsell their competitors by 20 percent. These gains are understandable when 88 % of consumers say they're more likely to shop with retailers that deliver personalized and connected cross-channel experiences (source: Swirl Networks).

In short, retailers can now communicate savings to each of their shoppers on relevant products, with a goal of winning the shopping trip and growing the relationship over time. Each of the 40,000+ sku's in the store is available to be promoted to each individual customer. The artificial constraint imposed by brand marketing funds is removed in the Age of 'i', allowing the retailer, once again, to realize the full potential afforded by truly catering to each shopper individually.

Contrast Age of 'i' marketing to what happens today. Mass promotions out of sync with each individual's purchasing pattern. Discounts that are either too little or too much for the specific shopper. Weekly mass promotions encouraging shoppers to go store to store to save money. All this results in massive waste and lost opportunity.

Imagine as a marketer the sales gain, promotion cost saving, and marketing efficiency that could be achieved by aligning promotional activity across all product categories to the purchase cadence of each individual customer. Or, think of the competitive disadvantage if a competitor like Amazon develops this capability first.

A few retailers are already moving in the right direction, albeit from a product-first perspective. Conversant in the language of customer identified purchase data, Ron Bonacci, Vice President of Advertising & Marketing for Weis Markets, looks at how many customer households typically purchase a proposed product promotion. An example he sometimes uses contrasts the impact of promoting strip steaks vs. ground beef. Even though each promotion may generate around the same revenue, the number of customer households purchasing the ground beef is far greater than the smaller number of households purchasing the much more expensive strip steaks.

Ron's reasoning is powerful. If ground beef generates the same sales dollars as strip steaks yet gets three times the number of customer households in the store, where they will purchase other products, advertising ground beef is the preferable promotion when trying to reach more customers. What Ron is really doing is increasing the relevancy of Weis to more shoppers, seeking to grow the customer relationship by providing savings on a product valued by a greater number of shoppers.

State of the Art: Marketing Personalization Built for Retail in the Age of 'i'

To power up retail marketing in the Age of 'i' takes far more than AI and machine learning technology. Vast attribution - of shoppers, of products, and more, as we'll see ahead - is the fuel. Deep integration into digital touchpoints is required to provide realtime relevancy. Location drives contextual relevancy.

Birdzi is an example of a solution provider built for Age of 'i' retail marketing. Their personalization engine calculates and maintains hundreds of attributes for each individual customer, updated with each purchase. And Birdzi can ingest hundreds, even thousands, of additional attributes from multiple sources all with a goal of building a relationship with each customer through relevancy.

Addressing a common failing at retail, the relevancy is supported across every digital channel, touchpoint, and engagement. Too often, retailers fail to provide this comprehensive approach, letting different personalization 'engines' power up different channels. That's like trying to build a relationship when only understanding every 10th word in a conversation.

Just as the retailer must start with the customer and understand what promotions are relevant to each, retail marketing in the Age of 'i' requires an upending of the promotion management systems and marketing capabilities that retailers have cobbled together. What's needed in the time ahead is a solid foundation, a comprehensive marketing platform encompassing promotion creation and management, sophisticated, realtime contextual relevancy driven by strategies to build customer relationships, and deep integration into digital touchpoints. Anything less leaves a retailer behind the curve before they even get going.

It's All About Mobile

I was attending a retail conference in 2001 when I was approached by a guy who looked like a mad scientist, think Emmett Lathrop "Doc" Brown, Ph.D., the fictional character in the Back to the Future movies. Jesse Quatse was a principal with 7th Street Software, a startup based in Berkeley, CA that was funded by Nokia's venture arm, and he had come to the conference to track me down.

What Jesse and the 7th Street team had built, and were so excited to show me, was the world's first automated, algorithm-based targeting engine for retail. Until this invention, the process of targeting offers to shoppers was a manual, iterative, list-based process. The engine 7th Street had built was game changing.

That 7th Street Software was funded by Nokia was telling. In a subsequent visit to Helsinki and meeting with Nokia executives, it became very clear that Nokia realized the implications of the growth of mobile phones and the impact they would have far beyond simply making calls. Nokia understood nearly 20 years ago that the mobile phone was a personal device and that the small screen demanded that any information, especially marketing, be relevant. And that required new tools that would automate content personalization on a massive scale.

Mobile, particularly the smartphone, is fundamental to Retail in the Age of 'i'. "80 percent of shoppers now use the Internet for grocery research, with 24 percent of that research done on a smartphone or tablet. Out of that group, 80 percent spend their time shopping through an app – a completely different way than she would have spent her time in the past, where she would have spent time in the store, picking up products, looking for ideas, and researching recipes in cookbooks."[18]

But the mobile opportunity is a double-edged sword. Using a mobile app or notification to simply convey mass promotions is equivalent to spamming shoppers. This is driving the growing use of mobile ad blocking solutions or the shopper simply deleting the offending app. If you're not providing value relevant to me, you have no place in my mobile.

Beyond using the smartphone to communicate contextually relevant information and promotions, many retailers use the customer's mobile phone number as a customer ID in lieu of traditional loyalty cards. This approach has enabled retailers to move beyond capturing household level data to the individual customer. Coborn's, a regional supermarket retailer based in St. Cloud, Minnesota, launched their MORE Rewards loyalty program using only the customer's mobile number; no traditional loyalty cards or key tags were ever issued.

And to be truly relevant on the shopper's mobile, this marketing personalization must occur at the individual customer level while accommodating household level relevancy.

My son has two young children. When he goes to the store he may *need* diapers, but what he *wants* is a nice Belgian beer. At the same time, his wife is on the Whole 30 diet while he loves carbs. The world today is all about having everything your way, and marketers would do well to heed that when thinking about personalization and relevancy. Ideally, when my son enters the store, he receives a notification that there is a savings available for him on the brand of diapers they frequently buy, along with telling him of a new Belgian beer he may like and providing an incentive to try it.

Buyer Beware: All Personalization is Not the Same

There are countless solution providers promising personalization, including traditional loyalty solutions, POS providers, eCommerce solutions, and more. But all personalization is not the same.

When considering the complexity and sophistication of state of the art marketing personalization, the skills and data architecture required to deliver it are often far beyond the capabilities of solution providers whose core knowledge is tied to their legacy capabilities. And attempting to build state of the art personalization and relevancy capabilities in-house is far beyond the ability of all but the very largest retailers. Retailers are strongly encouraged to do their homework when it comes to marketing personalization.

Strategic hyper-personalization has moved beyond yesterday's expensive consulting-based approach used by legacy solution providers into cloud-based AI and machine learning capabilities. These automate through software the ability to maximize the lifetime value of each individual customer by growing relationships through relevancy.

Personalized Pricing

Anyone who has purchased roses at Valentine's Day is familiar with product-based demand pricing. Because of the widespread spike in demand, purveyors increase the price of roses to what the market will bear (what customers will pay) to maximize product sales and profits. In similar fashion but on a more regular basis, most anyone who has been caught in the rain while visiting New York City quickly learns that the price of umbrellas seems to skyrocket until the rain lets up.

So most of us are familiar with product-based demand pricing. Richard Kestenbaum, in his Forbes article "Your Friend May Pay Less Than You For The Same Things You're Buying"[19] does a good job of explaining dynamic pricing and how it is quietly spreading into online shopping. Many of us have encountered dynamic pricing, such as when we fly; the price the airline charges based upon day of travel, when you purchase your ticket, your itinerary, and so on.

Consumers have come to accept dynamic pricing from airlines, hotels, car rental companies, and more. As Richard calls out in his article, the practice is spreading to internet retailers, where it is commonly referred to as cohort pricing. Rather than the price being based on travel related factors, cohort pricing is tied to groups (cohorts) of shoppers whose behavior is similar.

Effectively what online merchants are doing that use cohort pricing is communicating a price to you and other shoppers who resemble you.

Online retailers have available countless points of data on you as a shopper when you visit their site, including such aspects as if you're a repeat visitor, what competitor sites you've visited, what types of products you buy, and so on. Sophisticated online retailers tag shoppers with similar shopping behavior to a cohort and extend specific pricing to shoppers that belong to that cohort.

Personalized pricing in the Age of 'i' is used in service to the customer, providing meaningful savings on products relevant to each shopper. Some - many? - retailers will see personalized pricing as a way to maximize the number of shoppers in the store each week and to optimize sales and margins. But personalized pricing is really an arbiter of the quality of the relationship between the customer and retailer. The retailer wants to provide meaningful savings to the customer to foster and grow the relationship over time while the customer views pricing as one part of a broader value proposition.

Personalized pricing is already part of brick and mortar retail. Kroger has long used differentiated promotional pricing as part of its personalized marketing program. Albertsons-Safeway has recently started providing personalized savings as part of the company's Just for U program. And we're just getting started.

To compute, communicate, and deliver personalized pricing in brick and mortar retail requires sophisticated capabilities and systems. And these are being put in place by a growing number of retailers as you read this. Several years ago Kroger acquired KSS, a leading price optimization solution, and pointed the KSS data scientists at optimizing prices at the individual shopper level. This work is beginning to come to fruition as Kroger rolls out its digital shelf solution, enabling it to communicate personalized promotions and pricing to the shopper in the aisle.

Traditional retailers may love it or hate it, but personalized pricing is here and poised to grow fast as digital customer engagement grows and the physical store is increasingly melded into the digital world.

Beyond Promotions: Building Relationships with Personalization

Retailers in the Age of 'i' have vast opportunity to personalize the shopping experience beyond product and price promotion. As we'll see in a later chapter, health and wellness is playing an increasing role in the shopping experience as retailers like Kroger, Whole Foods, Meijer, and others give customers the ability to easily sort and filter the retailer's vast product assortment based on the individual's diet, lifestyle, or concerns.

Creative retailers can have a field day leveraging new technologies to recognize shoppers in the physical world. That means knowing that Mrs. Johnson is coming down the aisle towards the meat department, and surprising her with a bone for Buck before she even has to ask for it. Or the customer in the aisle being able to interact through text or voice to get immediate assistance or guidance to locate a sought-after product.

Retailer use of recognition and services tied to the individual customer can solidify and grow the relationship far more quickly and more substantially that promotions alone. Like my American Airlines example earlier, I'm sure that most readers can think similarly of businesses they frequent - restaurants, dry cleaners, auto repair, etc. - because these places recognize you or provide you exemplary service. In the Age of 'i', retailers can use new capabilities to bring that experience to each and every customer.

So we have seen that retailers today have game-changing capabilities to personalize the marketing and shopping experience with a goal of fostering a real relationship with each customer. Customers not only value this kind of interaction, they are increasingly expecting it. What's holding retailers back?

The Personalization Gap

Remember the innovation gap discussed earlier? The technological capability to work at an individual customer level is available to retailers today. It is the retailer's internal culture that is often the impediment.

Marketing personalization provides a case in point. Nearly all retailers are comfortable with the idea of taking the weekly ad containing a couple hundred items and filtering through it, communicating a handful of items most relevant to the individual customer. That's easy because it doesn't disrupt any established process. The retailer is still doing the weekly ad, just adding on the personalization element.

But how about this: If you as the retailer are digitally engaged with a good percentage of all your customers, remove the hundreds of TPR (temporary price reduction) signs throughout the aisles and communicate the ten most relevant TPR deals to each individual customer. You can now direct the right discount to the right customer and save countless dollars in subsidizing a product sale you were going to get anyway.

Or even this: Greatly reduce, or even do away with the mass printed and distributed weekly ad. Instead, provide a savings on the ten most relevant products for each customer drawn from the entire store assortment.

I can hear readers' hearts stopping.

This is what I mean about the importance of an innovation culture. Amazon is not locked into a 'we've always done it this way' philosophy. For Amazon and countless other startups looking to disrupt a massive industry - one that is ripe for disruption by the way - the goal is to think outside the box, to succeed precisely by doing things that the staid competition will not do. And as we saw in the previous chapter, this is the long game that Amazon is playing.

Some retailers are aware of the personalization gap and the importance of reclaiming a customer focus, regardless of retail format. Chris Leevers and his brother John own a number of Save A Lot stores, and were among the earliest retailers to operate the limited assortment, low price format. Over the years the Leevers family has operated other retail banners, including stores with a loyalty program. Knowing the value of customer data, and understanding the need to stay relevant to their shoppers - even in a limited assortment, low price format - has led Chris to exploring how to bring digital engagement driven by personalization and relevancy to his shoppers. No format is immune to disruption in the Age of 'i'.

CHAPTER 6

The Age of Customer Intelligence

So what does it take to really know each and every one of our customers? How can the associates in the meat department in store number 347 know that Mrs. Johnson is coming down the aisle and that her dog Buck loves a fresh bone? Or that Ben just entered the store and today is Saturday when he often buys steaks, which he likes cut extra thick, to grill out over the weekend?

To power up this kind of contextual relevancy and hyper-personalization takes enormous customer intelligence, big data brought together from many sources to provide actionable insights and attributes. Customer purchase data is only the beginning. Third-party data provides demographic, lifestyle, and economic data; location data powers contextual relevancy; increasingly detailed health data informs guidance to beneficial products, and realtime views to the customer's shopping list provide intent.

Big data is powering the Age of 'i', and retailers not understanding the importance of having, understanding, and using data are soon to be left in the dust. "According to an

Accenture study, 79% of enterprise executives agree that companies that do not embrace Big Data will lose their competitive position and could face extinction."[20]

The growth of big data is staggering. "90% of the world's data has been created in the last two years alone and the volume of data created by U.S. companies alone each year is enough to fill ten thousand Libraries of Congress."[21] "Some 2.5 quintillion bytes of data are created every day — a massive amount. If 2.5 quintillion pennies would be laid out flat, they would cover the Earth five times."[22]

The growing volume and velocity of data is one challenge; the proliferation of data sources is another.

Data has long powered modern retail, helping Walmart become a master of supply chain logistics and fueling Kroger's customer-centric strategy. Artificial intelligence and the cloud are fueling explosive growth in retail big data - and transforming customer marketing and many other optimization challenges. And as the retail industry moves online and customer digital engagement is the battlefield, the quality and quantity of data will determine the winners and losers.

And there is no time to lose. Tom Davenport, the President's Distinguished Professor in Management and Information Technology at Babson College, a research fellow at the MIT Initiative on the Digital Economy, senior adviser at Deloitte

Analytics, and the author of over a dozen management books, is more direct in his assessment. In a recent HBR article, "Why Companies That Wait to Adopt AI May Never Catch Up." Davenport calls out that AI is so game-changing that companies holding off implementing the technology, thinking instead they can be 'fast-followers', are instead putting themselves at risk because first-movers can create an insurmountable lead.

This new world requires - *more than ever* - data discipline. And this is an area that is particularly challenging to smaller retailers and even some regional chains. Data discipline will make or break retail success from this day onward. Here are just a few examples of issues I've encountered in talking with retailers:

- <u>Product Descriptions:</u> One retailer still had super abbreviated product descriptions that were used years ago with the old (much narrower) receipts. Product descriptions coming from the retailer's item file are used to power online shopping - abbreviated descriptions just won't do it for eCommerce as customers won't understand what the product is.

- Product Categorization: Another retailer's item file lacked any kind of product categorization on nearly 50% of the products carried. Many retailers lack even somewhat accurate product graphics. Retailers with these issues cannot realistically install any kind of marketing personalization capabilities that rely upon product categorization.

- Other Data Disconnects: Another well known regional retailer had many products at store-level that were not represented in item files at the headquarters office; i.e. the merchandisers and buyers at the corporate office did not know what products were in the store. This situation is simply frightening. How can a retailer do effective promotion planning and demand forecasting, let alone any kind of optimization, when HQ doesn't know what products are in each store?

Data quality issues such as these come back to haunt retailers when they look to deploy new capabilities like online shopping, promotion optimization, or marketing personalization - capabilities that are rapidly becoming a cost of entry to compete. And these are issues with what should be basic levels of data required to operate.

It's helpful to think of big data in different buckets tied to the source. In the retail industry, we have five primary buckets of data that retailers should be concentrating on. They are:

- **Human data:** This would include the usual PII (personally identifiable information) like name, email, address, phone, etc. Increasingly though, this will also include health related data, prescription data, data generated by wearables like the Apple Watch, and more.

- **Product data:** Product data is exploding, increasingly containing far more granular nutritional data for food products, including health and wellness related attributes like gluten-free, vegan, keto-friendly, and so on. Product data is also expanding to include sourcing data, transparency information, and sustainability data.
- **Purchase profile data:** This includes calculated scores driven by customer purchase data such as brand loyalty scores, discount propensity, purchase frequency, and far more.
- **Location data:** Location data today goes far beyond simple geo-fencing (targeting shoppers within one mile of the store for example) to include realtime location inside the store, and even customer cohort data that provides insight to where shoppers similar to the individual customer go other than the retailer's store, such as competing stores, restaurants, etc.
- **Third-party data:** This is data obtained from companies like Acxiom (now a division of IPG) or Experian. This can include demographic data, household income, education, lifestyle data, and far more. Many retailers use third-party data to understand the household spend on a retail category (like groceries) and then score the share-of-wallet they are getting.

Retailers face several significant challenges relative to big data: How to capture and collect it, how to store it, how to drive actionable insights from it, and, increasingly, how to make it available in real time.

Certainly, the growth of online shopping provides the ability to provide more personalized shopping. Many eCommerce solutions can provide access to the products last purchased, or most frequently purchased. It is also very easy in the online world to suggest wine glasses to the online shopper who just put a bottle of wine in her digital basket.

Increasingly, it is not only data powering up the intelligence needed, but it is realtime customer intelligence needed to keep pace with the customer today. For example, having a realtime view to the customer's digital shopping list provides intent, and an opportunity to present a related, relevant promotion, recipe, or other information. Likewise, knowing exactly where the shopper is in the store at that moment enables communicating relevant offers or information tied to the products nearby.

Customer identified transaction data is the bedrock of intelligence needed to power up marketing relevancy and personalization in the Age of 'i'. Knowing what specific products a customer purchases can easily power suggesting those products to the shopper whenever they are on sale. But this simple relevancy is only the beginning. Leading personalization solutions calculate and maintain hundreds of data attributes for each individual shopper, scoring brand loyalty, discount propensity, category behavior, frequency of purchase, and countless more.

Companies like Label Insight and ItemMaster are leveraging data science to expand the ingredient and nutritional information available for packaged products. This richer data is enabling retailers like Meijer to provide more relevancy, helping shoppers, for example, to easily find gluten free products. Each of the ingredients and health and diet related attributes for a product represent a new source of data that can be invaluable in serving each individual customer, not only related to health and wellness, but transparency in production and even sustainability.

As Big Data continues to explode, intelligence is flowing in from expanding capabilities. Sense360 is a young company that has assembled a panel of millions of consumers across the country to provide insight about where participating consumers' mobile devices are throughout the day. For example, Sense360 can help a retailer understand where else their shoppers go; which competing stores, drug stores, restaurants, are visited, along with the time on site. Alternatively, retailers can gain insight into the behaviors of shoppers in a given market who do not shop with them. All Sense360 data is consumer opt-in and does not gather any personally identifiable information (PII).

There are a number of companies using anonymous facial recognition to provide retailers an understanding of the demographics of their shoppers, including gender, age, ethnicity, even shopper mood (happy, sad, frustrated, etc.) at a high confidence level. Amazon's AWS recently rolled out Amazon Rekognition, a highly scalable, deep learning technology developed by Amazon's computer vision scientists to analyze billions of images and videos daily, and requiring no machine learning expertise to use. All a user has to do is use the Rekognition API to upload video or images.

Video analytics can inform a retailer of not only their shopper demographic, but also can provide valuable in-store traffic data, showing where shoppers go within the store and how long they spend there. Data like this is used by Kroger to project how many checkout lanes to have open in the next fifteen minutes and can even be used to measure service level effectiveness at different departments or areas within the store.

"At a time when customers can find almost anything they want online, brick-and-mortar stores must make it easier for shoppers to find the right products in the right place at the right time. Deeper, more powerful data analytics can help improve store design, floor plans, merchandise mix, and other elements of localization."[23]

Cloud based solutions enable retailers of all sizes to access cutting edge marketing personalization solutions driven by advanced data science to power relevancy across every digital engagement with each individual shopper. The cloud also brings sophisticated pricing, promotion, and product assortment optimization capabilities to retailers cost effectively. But the efficacy of these solutions is directly dependent on the quality and quantity of data feeding them.

Retailers embarking on data driven strategies would be well served to first assess the quality of their core data (product descriptions, categorization, pricing, product cost, vendor codes, and more). Retailers with loyalty programs should examine how clean and up to date their customer contact data is along with how customer loyalty IDs roll up to households (this area is particularly vexing as retailers often just distribute cards having the same ID number to members of a household, barring knowledge of the individual). Building on a now-solid base, consider bringing in third-party data to permit scoring share-of-wallet by customer household in addition to other attributes that can improve targeting and personalization.

More than ever before, retail success is driven by data. For retailers that understand the power of data - and especially customer and product data attributes - marketing nirvana awaits.

CHAPTER 7

The Age of Integration

My wife is a frequent Bloomingdale's customer and so receives a constant stream of emails from the retailer in addition to being a member of the company's loyalty program. We were shopping recently in a Bloomingdale's store when she recalled seeing an email promotion featuring extra points and discounts on certain brands, including one of her favorites. With that in mind, she found a couple of items she had been eyeing and we went to pay for them, only to discover that the special promotion was only available to online shoppers. Furthermore, talking with the store associate, we found that Bloomingdale's online business was nearly entirely separated from its brick and mortar stores.

This separation was driven home again the other day when my wife received a holiday promotion on jewelry. Again going to Bloomingdale's in search of a gift, we found an entirely different product selection available in the store vs. online. This is the antithesis of the seamless, omnichannel customers are expecting, and increasingly demanding, from merchants they do business with.

Bloomingdale's is a textbook example of a multichannel retailer, having an eCommerce store and physical store, but the two are siloed, having little integration, and offering different shopping experiences. Shoppers, though, do not see, nor do they want to understand, that distinction. In the mind of the shopper, Bloomingdale's is Bloomingdale's and the expectation is that the same promotions, brands, and product assortment will be available in both the brick and mortar store and online.

A study written up in the Harvard Business Review confirms that shoppers are indeed after a seamless, omnichannel experience. "We studied the shopping behavior of just over 46,000 customers who made a purchase during the 14-month period from June 2015 to August 2016. Customers were asked about every aspect of their shopping journey with the retailer, focusing on which channels they used and why. And they were also asked to evaluate their shopping experience. Of the study participants, only 7% were online-only shoppers and 20% were store-only shoppers. The remaining majority, or 73%, used multiple channels during their shopping journey."[24]

According to research firm IDC, consumers that shop both online and in-store have a 30% higher lifetime value than those who shop using only one channel.

Structural Impediments to a Seamless Experience

Consider this scenario: A retailer has regular and ongoing digital engagement with a growing number of its shoppers. This company is able to leverage all digital channels — web, email, text, mobile, even the receipt at checkout — to communicate a specific promotion to the individual customer. Powering this is big data customer intelligence: purchase history, brand scores, discount propensity, purchase frequency, seasonality, what items are on the shopping list, what items have been searched for, typical shopping days, time in the store, typical path through the store, time spent in different areas of the store, and more. On top of this big data is a system that leverages AI and machine learning to suggest the best promotion for a specific customer at the right moment designed to maximize customer lifetime value.

Many retailers are challenged to provide such a seamless shopping experience, held back by disparate systems and capabilities that have been cobbled together over the years as retailers were dragged into the digital age. Far too many retailers now suffer from capability silos. Their email is from one solution provider. Their website was either built internally or contracted out. Same with their mobile app, and other digital capabilities from other providers. This hodgepodge of systems creates a major structural impediment to providing the user experience shoppers expect.

And even when retailers think they have the problem solved, feeding personalized content to their disparate systems via an API or similar method, they're still missing out. State of the art today is an end-to-end digital ecosystem that provides a realtime view to customer intent - what item the shopper just added to her shopping list, what digital coupon was just clicked, what item was searched for - that informs what contextually relevant offer or information is provided back to the shopper in realtime.

The Importance of User Experience

Beyond capability silos that create structural barriers to a seamless digital experience, user experience is more nuanced... and something vastly under appreciated by a majority of retailers. Many executives have spent their careers advancing through the ranks of tactical, execution-focused retail, and they often approach digital capabilities as though it were a to-do list, checking off the requisite boxes. A case in point is the retailer who, knowing he or she needs a mobile app, signs off on an app provided by an existing partner, or whichever solution provider was in the right place at the right time. Maybe there was a short list of rudimentary 'must-have' features like a shopping list, or the ability to display available digital coupons, but no true review given to user interface and user experience.

And yet user experience is critically important. According to a Deloitte study,[25] 80 percent of surveyed shoppers have used a digital device to research grocery products, and 77 percent have used digital channels such as cooking blogs, recipe websites, and social media to learn about products during the awareness stage.

But many retail executives find themselves in foreign territory as retail success demands a shift from the product-driven past to a customer-focused future. While comfortable with supply chain logistics, in-store merchandising and labor efficiency, retailers are often challenged to appreciate the nuances of mobile app user experience, omnipresence via voice-enabled commerce, and automating replenishment of household goods through IoT technology.

Each of us, at one time or another, has gone to push a door open, only to find out it must be pulled instead. This is user experience at work. While that seems like a minor thing, small irritants like that in the digital world add up, and can lead to a user deleting an app or not returning to the retailer's website. Grocery retailers wouldn't dream of locating bananas two aisles over from the other fresh produce, yet there is no consideration given to the digital equivalent.

A retailer's website, mobile app, and other online experiences are the digital equivalent of the traditional store. In the Age of 'i' the digital experience is every bit as important as the physical experience in brick and mortar... and should be given the same attention to detail.

The User Experience Professionals Association defines user experience (UX) like this: "Every aspect of the user's interaction with a product, service, or company that make up the user's perceptions of the whole. User experience design as a discipline is concerned with all the elements that together make up that interface, including layout, visual design, text, brand, sound and interaction."

"True user experience goes far beyond giving customers what they say they want or providing checklist features," says Nielsen Norman Group. "In order to achieve high-quality user experience in a company's offerings, there must be a seamless merging of the services of multiple disciplines, including engineering, marketing, graphical and industrial design, and interface design."[26]

The importance of user experience cannot be understated.

- If your content is not optimized, 79 percent of visitors will leave and search again.[27]
- Mobile users are five times more likely to abandon a task if your website is not optimized for their device. (And two-thirds of mobile customers are looking to make a purchase that day, so you do not want them to leave.)
- Eighty-eight percent of online consumers are less likely to return to a site after a bad experience.[28]
- According to Adobe, 39 percent of people will stop engaging with a website if images won't load or take too long to load.

- One study showed that a well-designed user interface could raise your website's conversion rate by up to a 200 percent, while better UX design could boost conversion rates up to 400 percent.[29]

Kroger is focused on creating this seamless shopping experience, as Rodney McMullen, Kroger CEO, related in a recent earnings call. "Households that engage in our seamless offerings—engaging digitally and with our physical stores—spend more per week than households that do not," he said. "The future looks even more promising. We'll continue to add even more services, expand our available product selection, and more effectively use our insights to create a personalized experience that every customer will love."

Providing this kind of seamless - and relevant - experience requires retailers to take responsibility for all the content presented. We've recently seen a spate of activity around retailers seeking to monetize their web traffic by bringing in ads served up by third-party services. While this might appear to be easy money, it carries a risk when the customer is being presented ads for products or services that may not be relevant or of interest. Remember, every engagement will impact the lifetime value of the individual customer.

Need for a Complete Digital Marketing Ecosystem

Too often, retailers seek to cobble together a digital infrastructure from disparate pieces, trying to graft digital offers onto legacy merchandising and promotion planning solutions, and mobile experiences provided by responsive websites rather than sophisticated apps. Website providers and eCommerce solutions have long positioned themselves as digital marketing platforms but fall short. This plays out as a fast growing number of shoppers want to digitally engage but not necessarily shop online, and new capabilities extend digital experiences into the physical store.

Retailers need to focus on putting in place a comprehensive digital marketing ecosystem. Such an environment should ideally encompass the entire marketing process, including the creation and management of offers and promotions by vendors, a central AI powered 'brain' powering strategic campaigns and personalization across all channels, and deep integration into customer touchpoints providing realtime and seamless interaction.

Ideally, the platform can be opened to vendors — everyone from the big CPG manufacturers to regional brands to the local honey producer — to create digital content and promotions. Tied to a workflow approval process, retailers can bring into their digital ecosystem a vast array of promotions and content to be strategically directed to the right shopper.

By definition, all online shoppers are digitally engaged. But not all digitally engaged customers want to shop online. Online shopping is only one activity in much broader, more comprehensive digital engagement. Retailers must understand this key difference, and approach digital with that in mind.

It is only through this kind of ecosystem that retailers can provide the coordinated and cohesive user experience shoppers are getting from Amazon. Each product recommendation and promotion needs to be contextually relevant to the individual customer while aligned with the retailer's strategy for growing customer engagement and share-of-wallet.

Providing a seamless omnichannel user experience requires extensive and deep integration of systems, but there's more. To truly provide meaningful digital engagement, retailers need to think in terms of realtime data. And one of the foundational pieces retailers need in the Age of 'i' is realtime perpetual inventory at each store and each distribution center.

For the online shopper, finding out that one or more of the products they ordered were unavailable and either not delivered, or a substitution was made, creates disappointment if not frustration or even anger. Remember that the goal is to grow and maximize the lifetime value of each individual customer. Out of stocks, especially online, are a direct threat.

Surprisingly, a number of retailers have realtime perpetual inventory that is used to support demand forecasting and ordering. Itasca is one of the few companies that provide this capability. Talking with their executives, it is a no-brainer to connect that realtime product availability data to a retailer's eCommerce capability. Far better for a customer to know when shopping online that a product is not available and can choose an appropriate substitution, than find out when the order is delivered.

This disconnect is really part of a larger discussion around retailers' systems. Many retailers have brought different solutions in over the years that are used in different parts of its business. The result, as one significant East Coast retailer found, is substantial capability overlap, added costs, added complexity, and decreasing benefit.

Larger retailers would do well to bring in a world-class data architect to review existing systems and provide a roadmap to a more effective future. With Big Data exploding, a growing number of solutions available via the cloud, and sophisticated capabilities being made available through Amazon's AWS, Microsoft's Azure, and Google's cloud service, retailers can overhaul their platforms and position themselves for the future.

Walmart is a good example of a retailer moving in this direction. Earlier this year Walmart entered into an extensive five-year partnership with Microsoft to leverage its cloud platform and other tools to speed Walmart's digital transformation. The partnership is evolving quickly as both companies are co-locating resources at Walmart's tech center in Austin, TX to kickstart innovation.

As an example, Walmart recently rolled out an app to help in-store customers shop online. The idea is that if the shopper cannot find the product they are looking for in the store, a Walmart associate can help the shopper locate the item from Walmart online via the associate's handheld device, and place the order. The service will soon be available in all 4,700 stores across the U.S. And here's a real kicker: The shopper can pay for the online order when they checkout in the store.

This seemingly minor detail is actually very important. An estimated 15 million people in the U.S. are unbanked; lacking a bank account, debit cards or credit cards, and are thus prevented from shopping online. The new Walmart app enables unbanked shoppers to order products online and pay cash at checkout in the brick and mortar store. The ability to bring unbanked shoppers into the digital world of eCommerce has been a holy grail for Amazon and other large digital merchants. This new application from Walmart is helping advance the melding of the physical and digital worlds of shopping.

eCommerce in the Age of 'i'

As physical brick and mortar shopping melds with the digital world, customer experience is the defining battleground as shoppers engage with retailers at any time and from any place using different devices. This is about far more than just online shopping. New capabilities have come into the market that are transforming the shopping experience itself, especially in the store where a majority of retail sales continue to take place. Retailers can avail themselves of leading edge cloud-based solutions purpose-built to fuse together the digital and physical shopping experience, bringing new services and values to shoppers.

Primed by studies projecting 20% of industry sales moving online within the next few years, and triggered by Amazon's aggressive moves to grow its online grocery business, especially its acquisition of Whole Foods, supermarket retailers have rushed into eCommerce. The online frenzy has been further stoked by national competitors like Walmart and Kroger rolling out click and collect and home delivery of groceries across the country.

Aiding retailers are dozens of solution providers, many of them young companies rushing into what they see as a big opportunity as the massive grocery industry moves online. Nearly all of these online shopping solutions provide a complete, vertically integrated solution: shopping via web and mobile, order management, and fulfillment. Making matters even more challenging for retailers is that these solutions are rapidly becoming commoditized, providing little meaningful difference in the shopping experience or fulfillment operations.

And yet many retailers have deployed online shopping solutions, even letting the solution providers power up the retailer's website and mobile app. All with a belief that digital is all about online shopping. Except it is not.

Online grocery today represents an estimated five percent of sales with forecasts calling for up to 20 percent of industry sales to be done online sometime within the next five years. That means that 80 percent of sales will continue to happen in the physical store, where customers are leveraging digital as part of their shopping experience. And, "nearly all online grocery shoppers (99%) still shop in brick and mortar grocery stores."[30]

Reinforcing the notion that customer digital engagement extends far beyond online shopping, "51 percent of in-store grocery sales were influenced by digital technologies somewhere along the path to purchase, up from 33 percent in 2015, according to Deloitte Consulting LLP's "The Grocery Digital Divide" study. According to the Deloitte study, 80 percent of surveyed shoppers have used a digital device to research grocery products."

"Today, nearly 60% of shoppers look up product information and prices while in stores, and that number is going to grow next year. And now that augmented reality is available to hundreds of millions of iOS users across the globe, we'll likely see retailers and brands building more mobile experiences that overlay realtime information onto a shopper's surroundings in a store."[31]

The majority of executives have equated online shopping with all things digital. As the initial rush online begins to calm, retail executives find that the online shopping solutions they've deployed have created siloed, digital customer experiences. Even worse: Retailers are using third-party services like Instacart that completely disassociate the shopper from the retailer's physical stores and digital presence. While some retailers see using a third-party service as a way to move fast, the retailer is in reality walking away from the customer base they have spent years building in their brick and mortar stores.

Let's call this initial wave of online grocery eCommerce 1.0. But this siloed, digital experience is the antithesis of what shoppers today are demanding; a seamless, cohesive, relevant user experience across every digital touchpoint. Tech-enabled shoppers are tough taskmasters and retailers' first-generation eCommerce initiatives are no longer enough, especially for younger shoppers - digital natives - who have grown up in an Amazon world where product search and discovery are inherent parts of a seamless digital experience across devices and channels.

As a shopper, let me flag my favorite products, and then notify me when they go on sale, or if there is a coupon available. Help me browse your product catalog and provide me powerful search and filter tools so I can quickly and easily find the products I'm interested in. Then help me learn about the product's nutritional information, including more granular info than is found on the package. Tell me where the product is made, how sustainable the product is, and even the values of the manufacturer. Then, when I've found an item I want, let me decide if I want to stop by the store myself to shop, or send you my list to have the order ready for pickup later, or even have it delivered to my home.

Contrast this with today's typical digital experience where the retailer's primary website has no realtime access to the retailer's product catalog. Before the shopper can search for a product, he or she has to create an online shopping account or sign in to an existing account. That leads to laboriously searching through products, often using a department-category approach, only to find that many times the product catalog is not store-specific or has been reduced to a common set of items across stores. The shopper can put an item on the list - but only to purchase online for store pickup or home delivery. There's no option to add an item to a shopping list, because the online shopping site is disconnected from the primary site, where his shopping list exists. You get the idea.

Seizing the opportunity provided by comprehensive digital customer engagement means taking a different view of eCommerce. I am suggesting that retailers need to move away from eComm 1.0 towards a new model of retail, one where the digital world, encompassing online buying as simply one of many activities, is fused together with the physical store, creating a new shopping experience. Shopping in the Age of 'i'.

And this shopping experience is not limited to what products are available in the brick and mortar store. Some retailers are bringing an 'endless aisle' of products into online shopping, supplementing the store assortment with a long-tail of additional, slower-moving or more niche products that can be ordered online and shipped direct to the customer.

This next generation of online shopping separates the digital customer experience that is focused on product discoverability from the operations of fulfilling and delivering orders. The new experience provides the shopper a seamless user experience designed to foster product discoverability while giving the shopper options as to when and how they may actually get their products (shop themselves, click and collect, or delivery). This is in stark contrast to the siloed shopping experience of eComm 1.0.

The experience is powered by an end-to-end digital platform, everything from content (offer) creation and management to strategic personalization to customer touchpoints, leveraging state-of-the art big data architecture and cloud-based AI and machine learning capabilities to create the retail shopping experience needed.

One of the most significant challenges I see for traditional retailers is overcoming the cobbled-together systems they have put in place. These create structural barriers to creating the seamless, cohesive, and comprehensive platforms needed to fuze together the digital and physical worlds of retail.

And remember, if a traditional retailer doesn't move in this direction, Amazon and other digital competitors already are.

Coborn's is in the vanguard of retailers employing new sophisticated technologies to meld the digital and physical shopping experience. Shoppers are greeted as they enter the store, triggered by a beacon interacting with the Coborn's app. Knowing the store the shopper just walked into, the app automatically sorts the customer's shopping list by aisle for that store. The shopper is provided relevant offers as he or she moves around the store triggered by realtime location. Coupons are presented in order of relevancy, making it easy for the shopper to find savings on preferred products. And Coborn's shoppers can make use of a product locator function in the app, easily finding products in the store via a Google map-like capability. And does that heavy focus on digital work? Coborn's customers that are digitally engaged *spend significantly more than non-digitally engaged shoppers*.

Hurdles on the Road to the Age of Integration

In talking with many retailers of all sizes across the country, along with a view into a multitude of solution providers, there are a handful of issues that seem to come up time and again that create roadblocks for retailers as they work to a more seamless and cohesive experience.

- **Solution providers not playing well together:** As retailers seek to connect the disparate capabilities they have to improve customer user experience or provide new services and savings, they often encounter different solution providers not working together well. I can share countless examples of solutions begrudgingly working to integrate to some other capability at the retailer's request. At the first hint of an issue, one company throws the other under the bus rather than focusing on what's best for the customer (the retailer).

- **Retailer unable to deploy needed capabilities:** One example I can recount is of an eCommerce provider having a provision in their retailer agreement that the solution provider had exclusivity around any kind of personalization capabilities... even though the eComm provider didn't have any personalization capability at the time!

- **Walled gardens:** I have observed some solution providers believing they can provide all needed capabilities to the retailer and creating obstacle after obstacle barring any integration to another solution. I've seen this most commonly with certain POS providers who, for example, bar the retailer from using a digital marketing platform or mobile app that is provided by another company; the POS provider refuses to do any needed integration.

- **Retailers being held hostage:** The example that comes to mind, and seen at several retailers, is the provider of digital coupons having control of the integration to the POS and charging the retailer an exorbitant fee for delivering its own digital coupons and offers to its customers.

CHAPTER 8

The Age of Immersive Shopping

Anyone that has shopped at a newer Wegmans store understands what an immersive, experiential shopping experience is. Walking in the primary entrance you are plunged into the vast produce department, a prodigious selection of fresh fruits and vegetables just waiting to be explored. The stores resemble a European food hall, massive selections of fresh foods and extensive prepared offerings; even an in-store cafe and restaurant. For foodies, these stores offer a magical experience with new gastronomical delights awaiting around every corner.

Contrast that with the majority of retail stores that all too often provide a utilitarian experience, and even that is hard to come by sometimes. When shoppers can just as easily order their weekly groceries or dinner tonight from a growing number of providers, the reasons to visit a brick and mortar store decline by the day.

This is certainly evident across many different retail channels. Anyone who has gone clothes shopping only to find the size or color of the product desired is out of stock understands the frustration provided by traditional retailers. Even Tiffany, the venerated jewelry store, suffers from this problem, as I discovered recently when shopping for a gift; the store did not have either the items I was searching for in stock or the correct size.

Is it any wonder, according to a recent survey, why nearly half of millennials say they'd rather give up sex than quit Amazon for a year?[32] The act of shopping either fulfills a need (I need food) or it satisfies an emotional need, such as socializing with other people or providing an experience. Amazon has excelled at fulfilling needs, making the act of getting 'stuff' ever easier; I can order online and it appears on my doorstep within two days, or even two hours.

Visitors to the Westfield Century City mall in Los Angeles are quickly struck by the social aspects of shopping. Westfield spent an estimated $1 billion and two years doing a massive renovation with the goal of making physical shopping as easy and enticing as online. From reserved parking spaces to private elevators, the mall operator focused on reducing 'friction' in the shopping experience.

"Today, malls need to be more seductive to get people to show up. So only about half of the three-level Century City mall is dedicated to fashion, with the other half split between eating and drinking and a range of other uses that have little to do with shopping. There is a sprawling Equinox gym with high ceilings and hardwood floors. There is Next Health cryotherapy clinic, where patients can stand in freezing chambers, and a more conventional UCLA Health Clinic offering medical care. Amateur pugilists can work out in Gloveworx boxing studio.

Early next year (2020) the mall is expected to get the flagship location of Dreamscape Immersive, a virtual-reality entertainment center financed in part by director Steven Spielberg and AMC Entertainment, which operates the center's theater complex."[33]

Visitors to the mall will also be struck by the quantity and quality of spaces throughout the complex to sit and relax, enjoy an outdoor fireplace, play a game of chess, or have a coffee. Westfield is seeking to create the modern-day equivalent of the town square.

Returning to the supermarket channel, Niemann Foods' new Harvest Market store provides a great example of how a regional retailer can leverage its historical community-based relationships to take food retailing in an exciting direction. Niemann's partners with local farms to not only sell local products, but to educate and inform shoppers through story-telling. For example, the store includes a "microchurnery" operating in full view of the shoppers, using sweet cream from a small local farm to start the process. The buttermilk goes into the biscuits made in the bakery and served in the restaurant.

Rich Niemann Jr., CEO, describes the store as a mission dedicated to connecting people back to the land, helping shoppers understand the sacrifice, wholesomeness, craft, and expertise associated with the local producers behind the products."[34] Delivering this kind of shopping experience is not easy to do. The Harvest Market store has a different culture, and the Niemann Foods team works hard to keep it separate from their other, more traditional, stores.

'Retail is not dead, bad retail is dead' is a saying making the rounds today. When shoppers can avail themselves of a multitude of providers to have any product they desire delivered to their doorstep, increasingly able to place their order simply by voicing it, brick and mortar retailers must provide a compelling reason to go to the store.

Digital Immersion

Project Nourished is an initiative growing out of Kokiri Labs that uses technology to transform the eating experience. "Project Nourished reexamines modern methods of dietary consumption by allowing participants to experience fine dining without concern for caloric intake or other health-related issues. By merging the physicality of molecular gastronomy with virtual reality, we can finally enjoy any food we want in a whole new way."[35]

The company uses aromatic diffusers, a virtual reality headset, a bone conduction transducer, a gyroscopic utensil, virtual cocktail glass, and 3D printed food that makes the participant believe they are eating and drinking whatever menu is programmed. For example, participants believe they are eating lobster and steak, along with drinking a beer, when in fact they are eating seaweed and drinking water. Project Nourished takes the idea of digital immersion to an extreme but shows just what can be done.

As physical brick and mortar shopping melds with the digital world, customer experience is the defining battleground as shoppers engage with retailers at any time and from any place using different devices. This is about far more than just online shopping. New capabilities have come into the market that are transforming the shopping experience itself, especially in the store, where a majority of retail sales continue to take place. Retailers can avail themselves of leading-edge cloud-based solutions purpose-built to fuse together the digital and physical shopping experience, bringing new services and values to shoppers.

"RBC Capital Markets predicts that Amazon's Alexa will bring in $10 billion in e-commerce revenue by 2020. "It's not a matter of if voice will be used as a brand and marketing advantage, but when," said Robert Blatt, CEO of MomentFeed. "And when that shift happens—moving from voice search to voice engagement—retailers want to have a first-mover advantage, as users only hear the No. 1 recommendation."[36]

Augmented reality is making its way into a growing number of retailers' apps, amongst them, Lowe's, IKEA, and Lego. Marketers are making use of Apple's ARKit and Google's ARCore to create AR experiences both in the store and elsewhere. "Adidas recently leveraged AR to sell limited-edition sneakers at ComplexCon in California. The group used AR to place its limited edition shoe drops around the convention center, with users pointing their phones at the AR-powered signs, unlocking some of the hottest kicks of the year."[37] There are endless possibilities for retailers to weave AR experiences into both online and in-store shopping to create fascinating experiences.

Alongside AR is Virtual Reality which is at last coming on strong, due in good part to the cost of VR headsets coming down. The Oculus Go headset starts at $199, opening up a vast market. As computer processing power continues to become more powerful and ever-cheaper, the ability to create realistic and compelling shopping experiences inside VR grows. Anyone who has experienced VR can begin to understand the power of this.

While AR and VR experiences are becoming more widespread, Carnival Cruise lines provides a glimpse into the future of how to meld the physical and virtual worlds to create immersive experiences while providing valuable new services. Carnival's efforts revolve around its Ocean Medallion, a sort of Disney MagicBand for the cruise ship. The medallion is a wireless device about the size of a quarter that is provided to each cruise-goer a week or two before departure. The device can be a wearable using a watch-type strap, a necklace, or just carried loose.

After receiving the medallion, the cruise-goer goes online to register the device and create their account, noting food preferences, relationship to other family members going on the cruise, and can create a digital wallet containing payment vehicles. Once onboard, the medallion is the key to a vast number of services throughout the ship.

It acts as a wireless key to open your cabin door. It automatically communicates your food and drink preferences to the waitstaff as you enter the bar or dining room. Using one of the many large digital screens throughout the ship, family members can locate each other through onboard location services. And the list goes on.

Some brick and mortar retailers already have some of the infrastructure in place to begin tailoring the physical shopping experience to the individual customer; rather than a medallion, the customer's smartphone is the key.

Niemann Foods County Market stores greet each customer as they enter the store, the greeting triggered by a bluetooth beacon positioned at the entrance. The beacon interacts with the retailer's app through a cloud-based solution provided by a technology partner.

But this capability can do much more. The customer's usual deli order is easily surfaced from all the purchase data available - its an easy step to pinging the customer as they enter the store if they would like their usual deli order prepared while the customer shops, and they can just stop by and pick it up. Similar to Carnival's understanding of food allergies and preferences, a food retailer can be notified of food allergies or preferences as the customer approaches the prepared foods area.There is no end to how technology can be leveraged to provide more services but to also deliver a more immersive experience.

Power of Discovery as Part of Experiential Shopping

Many retailers, certainly supermarkets, have long relied on the power of impulse purchasing to grow basket size and customer spending. One of the oft heard challenges in the transition to online shopping is how retailers create the digital equivalent of impulse buying. While important, I would suggest that impulse purchases are part of a much bigger story: Discoverability.

Discoverability encompasses how shoppers are able to easily and efficiently find the products they know they want. It also encompasses helping the shopper discover products they didn't know about. Think of it as providing some element of surprise and delight within each shopping engagement, be it in the physical store or in the online world.

Millennial shoppers have been a particular focus of retail marketers over the past several years as study after study calls out that this generation shops far differently than older shoppers. For example, for millennial shoppers it is regular behavior to go online - usually from a smartphone - to research specific products either while in the aisle or before the trip. While many shoppers will research a more expensive purchase (eg. computers, appliances, etc.), millennial shoppers will go online to research a granola bar.

I believe this kind of 'research-driven' shopping behavior is becoming more widespread across shoppers of all age groups including, surprisingly, older shoppers. Consider for a moment that shoppers of any age are spending more and more time online, including shopping online where searching for a sought-after product is normal behavior. In the world of food retailing, a significant number of shoppers today have food allergies, lifestyle preferences, are on some diet, or have medical conditions that require avoiding and consuming specific foods. All of that lends itself to wanting to learn about and understand the products a retailer sells; and especially if the product that I'm interested in is on the shelf in the store I intend to visit.

Think of this in terms of path to purchase. A growing number of shoppers want to research a product before buying, and this can happen inside or outside the store. Once the shopper finds a product of interest, they then make the decision to add it to their shopping list or add to their online order. For shoppers doing this research at home or on the go, the ability to research products often dictates the store visit. In other words, retailers not providing this product discoverability will risk losing shopping trips from a growing number of shoppers.

Beyond Product Discovery: Transparency and Sustainability

Millennial shoppers are motivated by company and product values. "A lot of millennials are geared by the values of the production instead of the value of the product. They want to know who is producing it and where is it coming from."[38] According to the FMI Trends 2017 report, millennial shoppers want to support companies that share their values.

Closely related is sustainability. Retailers who can provide information about sustainability efforts earn points from millennial shoppers. The importance of sustainability extends to products; if there is a sustainability story behind a certain product or brand, this can become a deciding factor in the purchase decision, often outweighing price.

Making Discovery Part of Experiential Shopping

In the digital world, it's easy to present a digital ad alongside a product the shopper just added to his or her virtual cart. Retailers can also leverage state of the art marketing personalization capabilities to present relevant digital ads, offers, notifications, and information across their websites, mobile apps, email, and other digital channels. This kind of activity may not be easy, but it is certainly do-able with technologies available today.

Far harder is bringing that kind of discovery into the physical shopping experience and adding an element of 'surprise and delight' to discovery online or in the store.

The growing use of digital signage provides one vehicle for discovery, especially when it is linked to the nearby shopper. Kroger's Edge, the digital shelf signage being rolled out, lends itself to this scenario. Kroger, leveraging the vast intelligence it has on its customers, has the ability to light-up a product as the customer is walking down the aisle, drawing attention to a new item that may be of interest or special deal just for that shopper.

Department stores like Nordstrom have long used clienteling solutions to foster customer relationships. Nordstrom recently acquired BevyUp, a digital capability that will be included in a new integrated mobile employee app Nordstrom is rolling out this year. The app will help the employee make product suggestions based on knowledge of the customer's past purchases and provide a more complete omni-channel experience.

Technology in Service to the Customer

I recently visited Nike's flagship store on 5th Ave in New York City. Stretched across five floors, the store was blanketed in digital screens in every direction. Some of those were in support of customizing Nike shoes; a shopper can choose to customize many parts of the shoe while they wait.

Near the entrance were lockers where a product ordered online can be picked up by the shopper on their way by; no interaction with Nike staff required. Upstairs, shoppers are encouraged to download the Nike App. After finding a pair of shoes, they can order the correct size through the app, and the product will be brought out to them. The app also enables shoppers to scan their product and pay, no need to stand in a checkout line.

The store was working hard to use technology to make shopping easier and providing many options for customers. But it was also almost overkill, to the point of needing sunglasses to calm the glare of so many screens. What the Nike store is missing, in my opinion, is humanness; it is not about connecting with a shopper and building relationships. It is very transaction-focused, albeit very convenient transactions, using technology to help the shopper discover and obtain the product they are interested in.

The retailers who will succeed going forward will leverage technology in service to creating rich, immersive shopping experiences that are tuned to the individual customer. They need to know, in every store, that Mrs. Johnson is coming down the aisle and to have Buck's bone wrapped up and waiting with a bow on it.

CHAPTER 9

The Age of Innovation

Typing 'innovation' into Google's search bar returns over 2 billion results. Some would say that innovation has become an overused buzzword. The trouble is that the word, or something that means the same thing, is needed, especially today. As we saw earlier, the pace of tech-fueled change is escalating and we now live in a world of continual change driven by new capabilities. Like it or not, we live in the Age of Innovation and there's no going back.

There is no better example of how a traditional supermarket retailer must change to remain competitive in today's world than that provided by Kroger. As the grocery industry moves online and is confronted by new competition, Kroger is becoming as much a technology company as it is a grocery retailer. Other retailers like HEB and Ahold are investing heavily in digital, new innovation centers, and partnering with universities to explore use of artificial intelligence in retail.

And while technology innovation and consumer adoption of new technology have gotten faster, retailer adoption of new capabilities has remained flat. We have actually seen some retailers slowing adoption of new innovation, overwhelmed by the breadth and pace of change.

"Companies are iterating not in years but in days," Groom (Kroger Technology's General Manager) said. "We're in a digital arms race. We're a 133-year-old grocery chain that's competing with companies that didn't exist a year ago." (Source: Cincinnati Business Courier)

The challenge for retailers is learning to adapt to this new world, a world where they no longer necessarily drive new capabilities or services; often, it is consumer adoption of new technologies that retailers must respond to. I would suggest, given the scope and impact of new technology-enabled capability, that retailers of all sizes would do well to develop and implement strategies and processes for managing innovation.

Step #1: Gaining Awareness of New Innovation

What I am suggesting is a formalized process for learning about new innovation, filtering through the massive number of new capabilities flowing into the market each year, figuring out what to test, which to pilot, and which to ultimately deploy.

Remember where we are on the exponential growth curve. The pace of change driven by new tech-fueled capabilities, is increasing daily. The first challenge of innovation in the Age of 'i' is simply working to maintain awareness of new solutions and capabilities flowing into the industry.

Consider how retailers approach innovation today. Retailers have four paths they can follow. Here are the first three:

- The first path, which is not really a path at all, is to simply do nothing. And, frighteningly, there are retailers who bury their proverbial head in the sand, wanting to ignore the change whirling about them. These retailers are not long for this world.

- The second path, and one that a majority of retailers follow, is going to trade shows to discover what's new, in addition to relying on solution providers, calling them seeking to meet. This is the conventional approach to learning about new capabilities and, while it may give the executive some comfort that they have new innovation covered, only a fraction of what is being developed is coming to their attention.

- The third approach, increasingly used by larger retailers, is partnering with a technology accelerator or even venture capital group. Target's partnership with Tech Stars is a good example of this, and can indeed help the retailer discover and learn about new technologies and capabilities. But the problem is, again, it exposes the retailer to a very limited set of new solutions.

Many larger retailers are besieged by established technology providers and countless new startups bringing new capabilities to the retailer, leading some to think they have a handle on new innovation, when in truth they are seeing only a small portion of new technologies coming available. As mentioned earlier, Walmart's Store No. 8 team reviews around 700 new solutions each year; CART reviews around 1,000 new capabilities annually. And the pace is only growing.

Few retailers have the resources of Walmart to focus on gaining awareness of new technologies. To help retailers, the Center for Advancing Retail & Technology reviews and curates new solutions, making them available as a resource through its site, advancingretail.org, for retailers to search for, discover, and learn about new capabilities.

Which brings us to the fourth path: CART has partnered with GMDC's Retail Tomorrow group to provide an Innovation Program for larger retailers, wholesalers, and brand manufacturers. The CART team works with the retailer's executive team to understand areas of challenge and interest, then brings together the most appropriate leading edge capabilities for an on-site event at the retailer's headquarters where the executive team can learn about new technologies.

In addition, the CART team draws on its unique experience to watch for Black Swans, new capabilities that are not on anyone's radar that have the potential to be truly game-changing.

When retailers are reviewing new capabilities or technologies to consider for pilot or deployment, the first question that should be asked is 'how does this help us focus on the individual customer? How does this new capability clearly help us acquire, grow, and retain customers?' Remember, acquiring, growing, and retaining each individual customer is the beacon guiding the retail organization as it moves forward. Without that guiding light, it is very easy to become lost in the maelstrom of exciting new innovation and go chasing after the next shiny object.

The connection between new innovation and the individual customer may not always be direct. For example, the use of robots in the store are growing quickly. Some are designed to move up and down the aisles, monitoring for out-of-stock products, planogram discrepancies, pricing errors and more. Then there are automated floor cleaning machines, self-guided robotic floor cleaners that can be turned loose when the store is quiet. In both these scenarios, automation is helping grow sales and margin by addressing out-of-stocks in a timely manner, or reducing labor costs. Some portion of the gain or the savings can be redirected to improve staffing levels to provide better customer service. And that improved service can positively impact individual customers.

Step # 2: Create A Culture of Innovation

Retailers tend to be more tactical and execution focused; discover a problem or opportunity and fix it. We see this approach being applied to new innovation over and over again across retailers of all sizes. The problem is this: Retailers quickly max out their resources trying to pilot and deploy new technologies and quickly discover that there's no end to new capabilities coming into the market. Quite the opposite: The pace of new capabilities is growing ever-faster.

This jamming up of resources inevitably leads to a form of 'hurry up and wait' as executives learn about and commit to some new technology or solution but then find that their plate is already full and the new capability is put on a back burner for a few months until they can get to it. Given the increasing pace of exponential growth, that back burner better be getting bigger too.

Instead, we encourage retailers to step back and focus on developing a true culture of innovation, beginning with the senior executive team. The goal is to help executives understand what gets in the way of new innovation and learning how to break through those barriers.

Sometimes fear is a great motivator. Many retail sectors, grocery retailing in particular, have been notoriously slow moving. This has changed recently as retailers have had no choice but to move online and begin to test and deploy new technologies to remain relevant with shoppers, to address new competition, and to match productivity gains achieved by competitors. But far too many retailers have been dragged kicking and screaming into the Age of Innovation. Far better is to understand the new normal and build a company culture that embraces new innovation.

One of the issues I regularly encounter, many times from senior executives of the many regional retailers based in more rural areas around the country, is the belief that their shoppers are less tech savvy, and so they don't have to worry as much yet about digital initiatives. I recently spoke to one such senior executive who, when discussing the importance of mobile apps and a seamless, comprehensive user experience, said that this company's shoppers are older and are in rural areas, and so digital is just not that critical yet.

That's hard to believe when, according to Pew Research, 95% of Americans owned a cellphone in 2018, with 77% of Americans owning a smartphone, and 42% of people over the age of 65 owning one. Pew also calls out that in 2018, 89% of Americans used the internet. Location is no longer a proxy for customer technology illiteracy.

Almost hand-in-hand with this is how retailers approach new capabilities. Many seasoned grocery executives have spent their careers being rewarded for following, letting someone else bring innovation to market and only following when it's been proven successful. Years ago IT executives would buy IBM, even if it wasn't the best choice, but because it was the 'safe' choice. This practice continues today as retailers sign deals with 'established' providers because they believe it is the safe choice, failing to understand that today's environment rewards fresh, forward-looking thinking.

Step #3: The Agile Organization

Agile is a project management philosophy often used in software development. Its characterized by dividing tasks into short phases of work, and uses frequent communication to reassess and adapt plans on a continual basis.

The Agile movement is increasingly being applied to organizations as a way to help companies adapt and succeed in the new world of ever-faster change and disruption. The easy way to think about this is to consider the traditional organization as a machine that is very structured and process-driven. And, like most machines, it performs well when applied to the task it was designed for but quickly breaks down when used for something else. A tractor works fine in the field but doesn't do too well on a race track.

The new paradigm is to consider the organization like a living organism, able to quickly respond to its environment. Similar to an organism, there is some structure or central system that maintains life and allows the organism to function while providing for adaption to the external world as needed.

Applying an Agile philosophy to retail organizations is not without its challenges but it does offer retailers a potential path to adapting their companies to the increasing pace of change, transformation, and disruption that is the Age of 'i'.

Growing Innovation is the New Normal

Remember earlier in the book the discussion around Amazon making 42 major product and service announcements in one quarter? That kind of capacity to create and manage change and innovation doesn't just happen. Amazon as an organization has worked to develop the structure, culture, processes, and resource allocations to make that happen. Over and over again.

Looking forward, the retail industry would be well served to focus on the three steps outlined here to develop a plan for how to survive and thrive in this new world.

Increase awareness of new capabilities flooding into the market.

Build a culture of innovation.

Move faster.

CHAPTER 10

Keeping Score in the Age of 'i'

A fundamental reason why the retail industry became product-centric is very straightforward: Products were the only thing that could be measured. Until recently, retailers have had no way of accurately measuring customers, but that is changing as eCommerce grows and retailers increasingly understand the importance of identifying the customer in the brick and mortar store.

Theodore Levitt was an economist and professor at Harvard Business School. He was also editor of the *Harvard Business Review* and well known for increasing the publication's circulation and reputation as a thought-leader. In his book, *The Marketing Imagination*, Levitt speaks to the importance of a customer focus:

> "Without customers in sufficient and steady numbers there is no business and no profit. No business can function effectively without a clear view of how to get and hold customers, what its prospective customers want and need, and what options competitors give them, and without explicit strategies and programs

focused on what goes on in the market place, rather than what's possible at the factory, the warehouse or what is merely assumed at headquarters.

"For people of affairs, a statement of purpose should provide guidance to the management of their affairs. To say that they should attract and hold customers forces facing the necessity of figuring out what people really want and value, and then catering to those wants and values. It provides specific guidance and has moral merit."

In short, what Levitt is advocating is that 'the purpose of a business is to create and keep a customer.' Making a profit is a requisite of business but it is not the purpose of a business.

Building on Levitt's definition of business purpose, I propose the purpose of a retail business is to *acquire, grow, and retain customers.*

That brings us to the importance of keeping score in the Age of *i*. Since the inception of modern retail, retailers have kept score by products sold. Retail has been organized around products, and product merchandising is typically an exalted role as it has been seen as the source of revenue and profits.

But just as technology is transforming and disrupting operations and processes across the supply chain, so too is it transforming how retailers are organized and, most importantly, how they keep score.

Peter Drucker: If you can't measure it, you can't improve it.

Retail executives know that that revenue - money - actually flows from customers purchasing products, but had no way to measure customer-based revenue; only product-based sales. This conundrum, though, began to change around fifteen years ago as loyalty programs began to take hold, giving retailers for the first time, a view to customer-based revenue. It was this customer-identified transaction data that opened the door to actually measuring customer behavior.

This customer-based data is the fuel in the Age of 'i', powering not only marketing, but informing nearly all other decisions across the enterprise. Retailers with strong loyalty programs, accurately identifying a large portion of their total sales and transactions, are well positioned. Retailers lacking this customer intelligence are already behind. Having customer-identified purchasing data has become mandatory for retailers, what's optional is operating a traditional loyalty program to capture that data.

While I believe that some kind of retail loyalty program remains the most efficient and cost effective means to collecting detailed customer data for brick and mortar retailers, it is by no means the only option. As eCommerce grows, retailers have, by default, detailed knowledge of who the customer is, what specific products they are purchasing, how often they are buying, and so on. There are other methods being used by retailers to capture customer data, some leveraging payment information to aggregate purchases, and some are more effective than others. The secret, and the power, of customer data lies in having enough of it. World class retailers have customer-identified transaction data corresponding to 90% or more of their total sales.

This is a place where some executives can get themselves into trouble, thinking that eCommerce alone will provide them the customer data they need. Certainly online shopping provides customer-identified purchase data; the trouble is there is not enough of it. Studies estimate that around five percent of grocery sales are done online today, and that is projected to grow to an estimated 20 percent within the next five years. That means 95% of sales are being done in the store today, and if a retailer is unable to identify those purchases to individual customers, they will be a casualty in the Age of 'i'.

Customer Data Provides a New Way to Measure Retail Success

If Retail in the Age of 'i' is all about engendering customer relationships, we need a way to measure the quality and effectiveness of our efforts. Customer-based reporting, including financial measures like lifetime value, become a proxy for measuring those relationships.

Every retail store and company has an ebb and flow of customers over time. New customers shopping for the first time, an existing customer base consisting of customers increasing their purchasing, maintaining their purchases, or declining, and lapsed customers. This graphic can help visualize this flow of customers over time.

The Customer Lifecycle

| New Customers entering customer base | Existing / Active customers | Customers declining in shopping activity | Lapsed customers |

Retailer's Customer Base

It has always struck me that retailers spend vast resources compiling and analyzing management and financial reporting based on the products they sell. They compare same store sales over time. Executives closely monitor department level sales, knowing that if they can realize more sales from higher margin departments, the gain will flow down to the bottom line.

This product-based reporting is inculcated into the very organization itself; category managers and store managers' bonus incentives tied to store sales and controlling inventory shrink.

What if a retailer brought customer-based metrics into their management and financial reporting? After all, revenue flows from customers, not products (I can't remember the last time I saw a box of Corn Flakes with a credit card!). Such retailers could report customer shrink (defection rate). They could reward management for improving customer retention or increasing customer acquisition. You get the idea.

Some retailers are already doing this. Ron Bonacci, Vice President of Marketing and Advertising for Weis Markets, has long known the power of customer data, having led development of Kroger's loyalty program early on. Ron uses a comprehensive customer scorecard to evaluate the impact of marketing initiatives and even operational activities. Rather than reporting by product category, Ron's scorecard measures the number of customers in defined, spending-based customer categories. He constantly measures customer acquisition (inflow) and customer defections (outflow). Ron's passion for customer data is contagious, as is clear to anyone who has met with him.

A scorecard begins by defining spending in a specific period of time. Note we are using absolute measures ($ spending) vs.

relative measures. While relative measures can be informative, there is always a top 10% or bottom 30%; relative measures do not provide a defined measure that can be used over time. The example below provides customer category or customer tier spending thresholds for a quarter (13 week period).

Customer Tiers: Spending thresholds based on customer spend during a 13 week quarter:

Tier 1: Those customers spending over $1,000 during the period

Tier 2: Those customers spending between $500.00 and $999.99

Tier 3: Those customers spending between $250.00 and $499.99

Tier 4: Those customers spending less than $249.99 during the period

Unidentified: Sales $ unidentified to specific customers

Once the definitions are created, a retailer can then report how many customers there are in each tier and the associated spending and shopping behavior. This essentially creates an inventory of the retailer's customers, and can look something like the one in the following table. The purpose of this is not marketing - so we are not looking at how many categories are shopped, etc. - but rather the purpose is management reporting. Just as you have an inventory of products by department or category, this is representing an inventory of customers by 'category' or tier.

Sample Customer Tier Report					
Period: Quarter (13 weeeks)					
	Total	Tier 1	Tier 2	Tier 3	Tier 4	Unidentified
# of Customers	12,000	360	1,200	2,040	8,400	n/a
% of total identified	100%	3%	10%	17%	70%	n/a
Sales $	$3,000,000.00	$510,000.00	$960,000.00	$570,000.00	$720,000.00	$300,000.00
% of total	100%	17%	32%	19%	24%	10%
Avg. $ per Customer		$1,416.67	$800.00	$279.41	$85.71	n/a
Avg. # Visits		28.5	19.3	11.6	3.6	n/a
Avg. Transaction Size		$49.71	$41.45	$24.09	$23.81	?

The true power of this approach lies in measuring changes to the retailer's customer inventory over time. Higher spending customers are proven to be significantly more profitable than lower spending, infrequent shoppers. Just like airlines seek to optimize the revenue yield from a flight by charging different prices, and retailers seek to optimize store, department, or category revenue by offering a different mix of promotion shifting the composition of a retailer's customer base can lead to improved profitability.

				Quarterly Customer Tier Summary	
Customer Tier	Tier 1	Tier 2	Tier 3	Tier 4	*Total*
% of Households					
Year 1 / Q1	1.66%	10.29%	14.32%	73.73%	*100%*
Year 2 / Q1	2.29%	10.71%	15.09%	71.91%	*100%*
Year 3 / Q1	3.06%	10.68%	14.75%	71.51%	*100%*
Year 4 / Q1	3.21%	8.98%	13.12%	74.69%	*100%*
Year 5 / Q1	3.44%	9.90%	13.48%	73.18%	*100%*
% of Total Spending					
Year 1 / Q1	10.32%	36.11%	26.14%	27.43%	*100%*
Year 2 / Q1	13.65%	35.47%	25.75%	25.13%	*100%*
Year 3 / Q1	18.15%	34.33%	24.07%	23.45%	*100%*
Year 4 / Q1	20.38%	31.42%	23.16%	25.04%	*100%*
Year 5 / Q1	21.54%	32.48%	22.55%	23.43%	*100%*
Frequency (Visits per Week)					
Year 1 / Q1	3.10	2.19	1.45	0.63	
Year 2 / Q1	3.22	2.29	1.60	0.67	
Year 3 / Q1	5.16	2.85	1.80	0.79	
Year 4 / Q1	4.56	2.73	1.72	0.72	
Year 5 / Q1	4.58	2.64	1.62	0.66	

Theta Equity Partners takes this idea to its ultimate conclusion. Co-founders Daniel McCarthy (Assistant Professor of Marketing at Emory University) and Peter Fader (Professor of Marketing at Wharton) have developed a body of work they refer to as Customer-Based Corporate Valuation (CBCV). In essence, what they are suggesting is that understanding, measuring, and projecting customer-related activity, which generates companies' revenue, should become a primary pillar of business valuation.

Theta's work to date in retail has encompassed a number of digital retailers like Wayfair, Blue Apron, and Overstock who, by default, possess detailed customer data. But in discussions with Fader and McCarthy, their methodology can be equally applied to brick and mortar retailers who possess significant customer data.

Where Theta's work leads is to using customer lifetime value as a decision-making tool across the company. Does a certain marketing activity, new product line, or new service help to increase customer lifetime value or detract from it? Imagine publicly traded retail companies in part being valued by their ability to retain customers!

When we consider large, publicly traded retail companies, Kroger is probably the best known for its use of customer data. Kroger has been collecting customer-identified transaction data across its many banners for over fifteen years. The company's focus on growing the value of existing customers has been a core tenet of its Customer First strategy for nearly that long.

The mainstay of Kroger's success is the strategic targeting of promotions to acquire, grow, and retain customers. As Kroger has grown share of customer, it has realized improved margins that have in turn been reinvested in key item pricing, helping the company grow market share. Improved pricing helps bring in new customers that are funneled into Kroger's targeted marketing initiative, starting the cycle anew. Kroger's customer strategy has created an upward spiral of value creation.

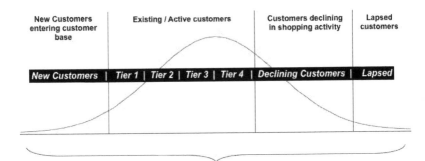

The Customer Lifecycle

Imagine now combining the insights provided by understanding the ebb and flow of customers through the store with the customer inventory and then connecting this to a realtime digital marketing platform powered by AI and machine learning. This kind of capability - and it exists today - gives retailers the ability to automate marketing to individual customers and the means to intelligently budget investment across shoppers.

Retailers like Ron use this kind of reporting to evaluate the efficacy of their various marketing programs and operational initiatives.

If Retail in the Age of 'i' is all about the individual customer, tools such as these provide a way to embed customer-based measures into a retailer's management and financial reporting. If we're going to live and die by the individual customer then, as Drucker said, we better measure what's happening.

CHAPTER 11

Organizing for Success

Many retail executives have given short shrift to the implications of exponential growth to their organizations. In a world of continuously increasing change, there are major considerations to both the organizational structure itself and how the organization operates day to day. Retail, indeed all businesses, was organized with systems and processes created for the world of yesterday, the world where tomorrow would look much like today. But that world no longer exists.

In the Age of 'i' it is time for retailers to upend the traditional structure and the way they have organized for the past hundred years. Technology is permitting retailers to truly shift focus from products, to individual customers, and the only way retailers will be successful with that transition is blowing up past practices.

Organization Structure

Retailers have historically organized themselves around products; it only stands to reason that products is what retailers measured. The rise of UPC level data and product scanning only embedded this product focus that much deeper into retailers' psyches. But it is time for change.

As we saw in the preceding chapter, retailers can now measure customer value, and indeed must measure customer value if they are to succeed in the Age of 'i'. This ability to measure customers creates the foundation for a new organizational structure.

There are implications to pay scales and incentive structures. Rather than tie a store manager's bonus to sales and shrink, consider tying the bonus to the percentage of more valuable customers in the store's shopper base and the manager's ability to retain those customers over time.

Organization and Training

eXP Realty is a publicly traded real estate brokerage and a rising star in its industry. Having a market capitalization value of over $1 billion, eXP's stock price surged over 300 percent during the past 12 months. The company has over 12,000 brokers, up from 6,500 at the beginning of 2018, and operates in over 300 markets in the U.S. and Canada.

"Incredibly, this growth is largely the result of eXP Realty's use of an online virtual world similar to Second Life. That means every employee, contractor, and the thousands of agents who work at the company show up to work—team meetings, training seminars, onboarding sessions—all inside a virtual reality campus.

To be clear, this is a traditional real estate brokerage helping people buy and sell physical homes—but they use a virtual world as their corporate offices."[39]

Stop to think about this. eXP has only a small physical leased office that is largely used for storage and as a headquarters mailing address. All communications, meetings, and training take place in their virtual world. Consider the cost savings involved, not just in office lease costs saved, but in the efficiencies gained relative to training. Instead of having to lease a meeting space, physically bring brokers together, and bear all the costs of that, eXP does all their training virtually.

Consider the time, effort, and resources that go into deploying a new system across your retail enterprise, be it one store, a hundred stores, or a thousand stores, and training your associates. It is considerable. Now think about how you approach this when that system becomes outdated in five years, rather than ten years previously. And then when you deploy the latest and greatest in five years, that system willl need to be replaced within three years. And then when you replace it at three years, its successor will need to be deployed in one year, and so on. And then replicate this across all the systems and operations of your company. You get the idea.

Walmart is turning to technology to help with the issue of training associates as new capabilities are deployed across the retailer's massive organization. The company has tested, and is now rolling out to all its stores, the use of VR tech to aid in associate training. Walmart is acquiring more than 17,000 Oculus Go VR headsets and distributing them out across its 5,000 stores for use in associate training. It is one of the largest VR-based training programs in the world.[40]

"Walmart US Academies senior director Andy Trainor explained that the method, which uses repeatable and scalable content, is effective because "when you watch a module through the headset, your brain feels like you actually experienced a situation." He added: "We've also seen that VR training boosts confidence and retention while improving test scores 10 to 15 percent -- even those associates who simply watched others experience the training saw the same retention boosts.

During its pilot test, Walmart used VR technology to train associates on how to operate the company's high-tech Pickup Towers. It'll likely do the same for other associates, seeing as it's adding 500 more towers the across the country by the end of the year (2018)."[41]

Resources and Skillsets

I was with the CEO of a large regional retailer not long ago, and we were talking about the key systems that were in place to manage the business, drive reporting, provide insights, and more. The CEO, to his credit, acknowledged two key challenges growing from the company's rush to stay competitive; they had deployed numerous solutions in just the past few years to address category planning, ad planning, business analytics, customer centric merchandising, and more. The first challenge was that, in stepping back from the frenzy of activity, the CEO believed there was a large degree of overlap between various solutions they had installed This created additional resource overhead, cost of maintenance, and added cost. The second challenge was coming to the realization that they did not have the right skill sets amongst their associates to truly use the new capabilities and get the promised benefit.

I have seen a similar scenario play out across a number of multi-billion dollar retailers. Management trying to do the right thing by bringing in the latest and greatest solutions but not understanding capability overlap and not appreciating the need for different skill sets.

Retailers would do well to develop a roadmap, projecting, as best as possible, where the ball is going to be in the next year, three years, and five years across key operational areas. All while understanding those timelines are being compressed by exponential growth of technology and realizing that we don't know what we don't know, that a black swan capability can come from out of nowhere that must be addressed immediately.

Retail success in the Age of 'i' necessitates speed and flexibility in today's fast changing environment. Some organizations get it and others clearly don't, hunkering down as if not wanting to acknowledge a new world and hoping the innovation 'storm' will pass. Except it won't. This is the new normal.

CIO: Chief Innovation Officer or Chief Interference Officer?

One of the key areas that I see holding many retail companies back is the very area that should be leading the charge: the CIO and the IT group.

In a surprising number of well known retailers, the CIO and IT team seem to insist on total control and final word on any new project or initiative that involves technology. The problem is that today, everything involves technology and, as we saw in the Age of Innovation, it is a Herculean task to try and simply maintain awareness of new capabilities flooding into the industry, let alone filter through them and decide which to deploy.

Beyond control issues is the notion that retail IT teams can build new required capabilities in-house. It is incredibly challenging for a retailer to have the financial resources, and even more importantly, the technical skill sets to build new, cutting edge, capabilities.

How can a retailer, unless maybe you're Walmart or Kroger. which are dedicating massive resources to new technology, hope to employ leading edge data scientists, AI and machine learning experts, specialists in pattern recognition, or world-class data and systems architecture? Consider, if you're a tech wizard conversant in AI or other cutting edge discipline, would you really want to go to work for a regional retailer, often headquartered in some more rural area, or go to work for a hot startup where you can have stock options, be surrounded by like-minded people in a fast-paced stimulating environment, and live in a tech haven metropolis?

Rather, I would suggest that CIOs evolve their role to supporting their company's needs around new innovation - let's begin to think of the CIO as the Chief Innovation Officer. CIOs have an opportunity to take point on helping the management team be aware of new innovation coming into the industry across all the different operational areas of a retail organization.

Beyond awareness, understanding the needs and opportunities across the various departments can help the CIO begin to work with fellow executives on filtering through the myriad solutions available to focus on those that offer the best fit. Part of this process is helping the executive team understand key trends and providing insights - as challenging as that is - into what's coming next. This can sometimes take the form of a near-term, mid-term, long-term roadmap.

Once a shortlist of solutions for a given initiative are identified, the CIO can coordinate pilots to prove out efficacy and improve understanding of what it takes to deploy and realize benefits.

Rather than focus on building technologies internally, the CIO and IT team would be better served to identify key solution partners, especially for core capabilities. A friend of mine coined the term 'technology putty' to describe core capabilities retailers need today. By that he means solutions that are architected to efficiently scale, can be delivered via the cloud or minimal hardware and integration requirements, and can be customized to the individual retailer. The secret is leveraging a common, scalable, robust core and then molding the interfaces and capabilities around the edges where retailers interact with and use the capability.

CHAPTER 12

iRetail Comes to Healthcare

According to Statista, the food industry in the United States, comprised of retail and foodservice sales, totals over $5 trillion each year. Nearly everywhere we look in the physical world—and increasingly online—food is available, including over 37,000 supermarkets, approximately 1 million restaurants, 150,000 convenience stores and more. You can grab a soda and snack as you explore Home Depot's cavernous stores, deliberate office supplies in Staples, or search for clothes at Nordstrom's. Food has never been more available.

While food has become pervasive, healthcare in the United States has become the most expensive in the world. The U.S. healthcare industry is projected to be a $5 trillion-a-year industry by 2023, representing nearly 20% of the country's GDP.[42] The Milliman Research Report 2017 states that annual medical costs for a family of four were $26,944. Healthcare costs do nothing but increase, as anyone can attest.

Our health is inextricably tied to the food we eat as study after study has shown. Tracing the history of processed, carb-rich and sugar-laden foods in the U.S. we see a clear correlation with the growth of obesity and chronic disease. The connection between food and health was clear more than 2,000 years ago as Hippocrates, the ancient Greek physician, proclaimed, "Let food be thy medicine and medicine be thy food."

And though they touch each person daily, these two massive, pervasive and intertwined industries are largely disconnected at the individual consumer. I often use the example of the person who goes to the doctor and is diagnosed with diabetes, is given a prescription and is told to exercise and eat better. That same person returns home to find a mailer from her local supermarket with specials on soda, chips and ice cream. Sadly, that story reflects the reality of food marketing today.

Many have tried to impact this important dilemma. There are countless third-party apps that attempt to provide nutritional data and guidance as to products being gluten-free, safe for diabetics, and so on. In addition are the myriad diet apps that seek to help shoppers identify products good for the multitude of popular diets that come and go. Where these apps typically falter is not being tied to the specific store's product assortment, so providing only limited value to a given shopper.

Supermarket retailers have worked to impact the disconnect between food and health, investing in health and wellness programs. Numerous retailers have placed dietitians in their stores as a resource for customers to assist with label reading, meal planning and to answer questions. Many of the same retailers have also implemented shelf-signage programs such as the recently announced Guiding Stars program at Ahold; products throughout the store labeled with a star rating that provides guidance to customers as to the nutritional value offered. But despite these efforts, the health our country's populace continues to decline.

A 2017 RAND Study, *Chronic Conditions in America: Price and Prevalence,* called out that 60 percent of Americans have a chronic health condition; 42 percent of people have two or more chronic diseases. The Mayo Clinic reports that 70 percent of Americans take a prescription drug and more than half take two drugs. "The nation is in the longest period of a generally declining life expectancy since the late 1910s, when World War I and the worst flu pandemic in modern history combined to kill nearly 1 million Americans." [43] Healthcare costs outstrip inflation every year. Estimates of lost productivity in the U.S. due to chronic disease are in the hundreds of billions of dollars. The lost quality of life is immeasurable. Food and healthcare are broken and must be fixed.

Programs such as Guiding Stars are being superseded by efforts making use of the vast data attribution possible today from companies such as Label Insight, which uses AI and machine learning to deconstruct the brief nutritional summary found on packaged foods to identify hundreds and even thousands of specific, granular nutrients, minerals and vitamins, found in our food products. This massive increase in available data is powering more evolved programs, such as that of Raley's, which uses the extensive data attributes to identify products as helpful for specific health conditions, identifying items at the shelf and in their online shopping service.

Key retailers are investing in new technology and leveraging expanded product nutrition data to enable a new approach, and putting more information in the customer's hands, helping the shopper to identify better-for-you foods throughout the retailer's stores.

Kroger is helping lead the way, extending its customer focus into health and wellness through its recently released OptUP app. The app provides a nutrition rating, on a scale of 1 to 100, for every product sold, and color codes products based on their score (Green are products with scores 71 and up, Yellow are products with scores 36-70, and Red are products with scores below 35). Users can sort products by a number of preferences, such as dairy-free, immune boosting, keto-friendly, or vegan.

Kroger makes it easy to get started, as we experienced firsthand. Living in southern California, we shop at Ralph's, the Kroger banner in our market, where we have been a member of their loyalty program for several years. Signing into the OptUP app with my Ralph's app credentials, the health and wellness app automatically pulled in our past purchases, scoring every item, and giving us an overall OptUP score based on our rolling past 8 weeks of purchases. In a world where relevancy is an expectation and health and wellness is increasingly important, Kroger's OptUP app is a great example of a traditional retailer leveraging technology to personalize the shopping experience.

Interest in connecting food and wellness is popping up in some unexpected places. Leever's, the operator of Save A Lot stores in Colorado, worked with a startup to create the Snap2Save app. Beyond earning points that can be redeemed for gift cards, the app provides recipes and cooking instructions. And through the Healthy Food Rewards program, shoppers earn four times the points for the purchase of fresh fruits and vegetables.

Efforts like those from Raley's, Kroger, and Leever's show that the food industry is stepping up and assuming a responsibility to provide information to customers to help them make more informed purchasing decisions and guide them to products beneficial to their health.

But even these efforts are being supplanted by a more personalized approach tailor made for the Age of 'i'. ScriptSave, which offers programs and services in more than 60,000 pharmacies across the U.S., is using granular nutritional requirements related to dozens of nutritionally sensitive health conditions to help food retailers position their stores as today's equivalent of Hippocrates' medicine chest.

According to Lance Jacobs, Vice President of Personalized Wellness for ScriptSave, "A majority of Americans are dealing with at least one health condition and are taking at least one prescription drug. A large portion of these conditions are nutrition sensitive and are significantly impacted by the foods we eat. Technology is making personalization ubiquitous and nothing is more personal than our individual health and wellness. And yet, with tens of thousands of product choices in a typical grocery store, the sheer number and complexity of those choices is overwhelming to the average shopper. At ScriptSave, we have connected health condition with those products (and their nutritional attributes) in order to connect people to "better-for-you" recommendations. Our vision is to improve health outcomes for millions of Americans while providing new value propositions and marketplace differentiation for the retailer."

The Personalized Wellness program uses customer self-identification (and can also use prescription data through a HIPAA-compliant process) to understand the specific health conditions, allergies, and food preferences of the individual customer. ScriptSave then uses leading nutritional data science along with sophisticated personalization to filter the 40,000 products across the typical supermarket, identifying those products that are beneficial to the individual shopper, and making those recommendations available via a retailer-branded personalized wellness app. Two significant regional retailers have already signed onto this initiative, planning rollouts in the coming quarter.

It is programs like ScriptSave's Personalized Wellness initiative that provide the foundation for what's coming next.

Realtime Health Data

Until very recently you had to go the doctor for various tests to detect and monitor a plethora of health conditions like diabetes, hypertension, heart disease, and many others. Today, people wearing the latest Apple Watch have a device strapped to their wrist capable of providing an ECG, able to monitor for heart abnormalities in realtime. Dexcom recently released a glucose monitoring device that communicates realtime data to your smartphone, providing diabetics with valuable data. TestCard, a UK startup, sells inexpensive test strips that provide clinical-grade urinalysis when read by a smartphone app. Users can monitor blood glucose, prostate health, kidney disease, STIs, and even illicit drugs. Omron just announced their Heart Guide watch, which provides realtime blood pressure readings.

"Presently, 33% of U.S. consumers have adopted wearables, such as smartwatches and fitness trackers, to play a more active role in managing their health. In turn, insurers, providers, and employers are poised to become just as active leveraging these devices - and the data they capture - to abandon the traditional reimbursement model and improve patient outcomes with personalized, value-based care.

Adoption is going to keep climbing, as more than 80% of consumers are willing to wear tech that measures health data, according to Accenture — though they have reservations about who exactly should access it."[44]

These kinds of technologies hold massive implication for food retailers. Imagine the shopper in the aisle being informed by a realtime glucose reading that directs them to purchase a specific product. Current health and wellness programs and dietitians would need to raise their games to add new value.

Food Retailers Can Become Trusted Partners

"In 1966, more than three-fourths of Americans had great confidence in medical leaders; today, only 34 percent do. Compared with people in other developed countries, Americans are considerably less likely to trust doctors, and only a quarter express confidence in the health system."[45] This decline creates a unique opportunity for food retailers to become a trusted partner in helping each of their customer's improve their wellbeing.

One of the byproducts of digitizing health records is putting more information into the hands of the consumer. I recently went in for an annual physical and, as part of that, had bloodwork done. Within a couple days of my doctor visit I received a message saying the results of my tests were available and I could view them online or through the Cedars-Sinai app. Looking at the results, I was able to see my specific score for a multitude of markers along with notes of how my score for a specific test compared to a normal range, and a suggested target for men of my age.

With information like this it requires very little effort for a consumer to go from a concerning health score to understanding what foods should be consumed. For example, the person going to the doctor and discovering that their blood pressure is high could then use ScriptSave's program to self-identify as having hypertension... and then being directed to specific products beneficial to improving hypertension found across the store.

Or, better yet, the customer can opt in and enable a solution like ScriptSave's to access the health records through a realtime API, making it even easier for the customer to be guided to beneficial foods across the store.

Convergence of Food and Health Accelerating

Looking across the landscape we are seeing a growing number of initiatives that are pointing to impending disruption in healthcare, and a growing ability to connect food purchasing with health data.

Amazon is at the forefront of this trend. The company's Amazon Web Services already houses a massive number of health records and recently announced it is unleashing its AI and machine learning resources on this data trove to assist physicians in providing improved care and lowering costs.

But this is just the beginning. Amazon acquired PillPack, getting the company into the pharmacy prescription business. It already understands what OTC (over the counter) products and medical supplies each customer purchases through its online shopping platform. Amazon can increasingly connect the dots, using your Prime membership ID to identify your food purchases at Whole Foods, Amazon Restaurants, and Prime Now with other purchase activity across their platform.

As a harbinger of what is to come, Whole Foods recently upgraded its website and mobile app to enable shoppers to easily filter products by a dozen or so preferences based on diet, lifestyle, and product attributes.

Apple enables a user to bring their digital health records into the Health app on the iPhone, where those records can be made available to an authorized third-party through an API. Opening up a potentially massive audience, "Apple is in discussion with the Department of Veterans Affairs to allow veterans to transfer their health records to their iPhone."[46] All this in addition to the growing capability of Apple's Watch to monitor key health indicators in realtime.

Google is helping move healthcare data to the cloud, organizing and opening it up to advanced analytics and insights and API access. That API access conceivably makes it far easier to begin connecting healthcare data with food purchasing data. And even Walmart is getting into the game, deepening its partnership with Humana, the massive managed care organization, with an eye towards a possible acquisition.

As a precursor to what's coming next, insurance companies like John Hancock are encouraging policy holders to share health tracking data. HealthIQ provides special rates on life insurance for cyclists who share their digital workout data with the company.

ScriptSave, working with its retail clients, is looking to bring healthcare providers, large payers, and managed care organizations into the mix. The idea is to create an ecosystem whereby the individual is incentivized and rewarded for improving the quality of foods he or she consumes.

The Future of Food and Health

In the Age of 'i', food and the individual customer's health are intricately linked, and customers will increasingly look to their food retailer for guidance on what to eat. After all, what's more personal than your health?

It is clear that the food you consume is inextricably linked to your health. As we've seen, the convergence of the health care and food industry is happening at a quickening pace. Personal health data along with food purchase data, and increasingly realtime health monitoring, is in the cloud, increasingly able to be connected.

Few would argue that this convergence and integration, used to help the individual customer discover, learn about, and be directed to beneficial food products, can provide significant benefit to the wellbeing of the individual. And health insurance companies have long provided incentives tied to increasing physical activity and more healthful habits.

What is a concern, though, looking ahead, is where and when incentives for more healthful eating cross the line to punitive actions. It is easy to envision a scenario in which health insurance companies or the government, which directly or indirectly funds a massive portion of the country's healthcare costs, begin to penalize individual consumers for enjoying potato chips instead of carrot sticks.

CHAPTER 13

Data Privacy and the Future of Shopping

Given that the Age of 'i' is powered by enormous amounts of data, much of it relating to the individual customer, it is incumbent on us to discuss data privacy. But a discussion centered on data privacy is a multifaceted issue.

Data breaches not only impact a retailer's bottom line, a breach can also negatively impact a retailer's reputation for years. As I'm writing this, Marriott International just announced a massive data breach of its Starwood guest reservation database, exposing the personal information of up to 500 million customers. The stolen data can include names, addresses, phone numbers, credit card information, and even passport numbers. The impact of this breach is still yet to be determined.

Marriott is just the latest casualty in a growing number of data breaches, many of them occurring at well-known retailers. "More than 16.5 million U.S. consumers fell victim to identity fraud in 2017. That's about an eight percent increase from the previous year."[47]

Beyond data breaches, consumers - and the government - are becoming increasingly concerned about the integrity of the big social media platforms like Facebook and the countless apps on smartphones that, unbeknownst to the consumer, are sharing confidential data.

Facebook has been particularly lambasted over the past year in regards to data privacy. The company admitted it was hacked several months ago, exposing the personal information of an estimated 50 million users. This on top of it becoming public that private information of nearly 90 million users was obtained by a British analytics firm, leading to worries that disinformation has impacted elections and even tied to deaths in several countries.[48]

Facebook continues to take hits regarding the confidentiality of data. For example, the company used phone numbers provided by users as part of a two-factor authentication process, to target ads. It has come to light that the company has had preferred relationships with key companies providing vast access to confidential data. All of this having a major impact on Facebook usage, which should be a direct concern of marketers as many retailers and brands leverage the vast social media network for targeted ads.

"Pew Research Center, in a survey released in June 2018, found that 42 percent of Facebook users have stepped back from daily activity and engagement. The study also found that

26 percent deleted the Facebook app from their phone. Over time, a less engaged Facebook population could affect how ads perform on the platform. Several agencies and campaign platforms have reported advertiser budget growth has stagnated on Facebook and accelerated on Instagram."[49]

Data privacy issues extend far beyond Facebook. A recent New York Times article described the incredibly precise location tracking data that many apps collect, some with user knowledge and acceptance, and many without.

"At least 75 companies receive anonymous, precise location data from apps whose users enable location services to get local news and weather or other information, The Times found. Several of those businesses claim to track up to 200 million mobile devices in the United States — about half those in use last year. The database reviewed by The Times — a sample of information gathered in 2017 and held by one company — reveals people's travels in startling detail, accurate to within a few yards and in some cases updated more than 14,000 times a day.

These companies sell, use or analyze the data to cater to advertisers, retail outlets and even hedge funds seeking insights into consumer behavior. It's a hot market, with sales of location-targeted advertising reaching an estimated $21 billion this year. IBM has gotten into the industry, with its purchase of the Weather Channel's apps. The social network Foursquare remade itself as a location marketing company. Prominent investors in location start-ups include Goldman Sachs and Peter Thiel, the PayPal co-founder."[50]

These issues and more are gaining the attention of the government, and there is growing discussion across not only government offices but technology companies themselves that data privacy issues are heading towards some kind of regulation.

While seemingly not as serious as data breaches and the unapproved sharing of confidential data, the proliferation of digital ads on every screen is causing additional issues. The use of cookies, bits of code that track a user's activity online, has grown to a massive industry as programmatic digital ad services harvest data about an individual's online behavior to serve up 'relevant' ads. This practice causes at least two significant issues. The first is that thousands of ads per day are being served up to a user across all their digital devices, including their smartphones. The second is that the ads served are oftentimes not relevant.

For example, I recently went online to purchase a new printer, doing research across several manufacturers sites, and then making my purchase on Amazon. For weeks subsequent to that purchase I was bombarded with ads for printers, even though I had made a purchase and was not looking to buy another. These programmatic ads were not relevant, they were annoying. To rid themselves of the annoyance of digital ads, over 24% of U.S. internet users employed ad blocking software on their connected devices in 2016, a number projected to grow to over 30 percent in 2018.[51]

Data Privacy: Interesting Times Ahead

All these issues around data privacy are driven by what has occurred. What is coming next is positively Orwellian.

Taylor Swift, the popular pop singer, used a facial recognition system at a concert given at California's Rose Bowl in May 2018. A kiosk set up at the entrance showed highlights of the singer's rehearsals; it was also secretly recording the faces of concertgoers which was being used to identify known stalkers of the pop star.

Driven by the increasing power of cheap computing power and advances in artificial intelligence, facial recognition use is exploding. Interest in the technology by police and government forces is obvious. Slightly less obvious is the use by private industry.

Look around in nearly any store or shopping mall parking lot and you'll find security cameras. Same goes for when you go inside the store; retailers have used security cameras for decades to control shoplifting and other incidents. Since those cameras are digital, it is easy to feed the images captured into additional software applications to provide additional 'benefits'. There are several companies that use anonymous facial recognition to provide demographic information to retailers including age, gender, ethnicity, and many more.

Similar capabilities are used to understand and track shoppers across shopping malls and inside stores, the goal being to understand store-level traffic, dwell times, and category purchase conversion, amongst other data points.

The growth of wearables like smart watches is opening the door to yet another area of data privacy. "Information about a person derived from wearables data such as the time, duration, and proximity of an activity to other tracked individuals combined with demographic information can provide crucial and detailed context to each individual interaction. Data gathered impacts how businesses market their products and how companies recruit talent and motivate their employees. Wearables gather a new class of sensitive data about people: not only who they are, what they do, and who they know, but also how healthy they are, what movements they make, and how well they feel. Heart rate monitors can provide insight into people's excitement and stress levels, and glassware can reveal exactly what they are seeing."[52]

Retail executives should be attuned to customers' psyches related to data privacy. Data is the fuel powering the Age of 'i' and has become mission critical for retail companies of all sizes. Given its importance, executives should have a firm grip on what types of data their company uses but also an understanding of any risk to future access of critical data.

Given the complexity of the issue, here's a framework to use in thinking about data:

- **First party data** is the information you collect directly from your customers. This includes purchase data, loyalty data, online data, mobile app data, emails, etc. First party data is gold, it is the highest quality data you can have in the digital marketing world.

- **Second party data** is essentially some other company's first party data that you obtain through a direct relationship. For example, a brand may have extensive data about potential shoppers in a given market area that go beyond the retailer's first party data; the retailer partners with the brand using that data to reach a broader audience to promote purchasing the brand at the retailer's stores.

- **Third party data** is data you purchase from data aggregators like BlueKai, Peer39, and eXelate, that collect it from various other platforms, websites, cookies, and so on. Large data aggregators vacuum up all the possible data they can acquire and then organize the data by segments based on industry, demographics, behaviors, and so on.

Given all the issues related to data privacy and confidentiality, the further removed you are from the actual source of data, the greater the risk associated with having access governed or even curtailed. For example, the growing use of ad blocking software bars the use of cookies to power programmatic ad buying. "A recent survey found that 40 percent of U.S. ad blocking is on laptops, and another 15 percent on mobile devices, and nearly half of all respondents stated that the intention to use ad-blocking software is to avoid irrelevant or annoying ads."[53]

In the near- to mid-term, retail marketers should be focused on growing the amount of first party data they have, especially direct relationships with their customers. Retailers that rely on second or third party data to power their digital engagement strategies are at increasing risk. If I were still a practicing retailer I would be focused on growing digital engagement with as many of my existing customers as fast as possible to lessen the impact of possible regulation. I would also focus on creating a strong value proposition for new shoppers to get them digitally engaged as soon as possible, even during their first shopping trip.

Looking to the future, there is a growing movement to give consumers control over their data. This is in part a response to the lack of trust and integrity on the part of social media platforms like Facebook and app providers, along with the growing understanding that the consumer data industry makes billions of dollars each year from consumers' digital activity.

"In today's data market, every purchase you make online, every website you click on using a browser, and each move you make that triggers your location can be sold by a company. Some 2.5 quintillion bytes of data are created every day — a massive amount. If 2.5 quintillion pennies would be laid out flat, they would cover the Earth five times. Most of the data is harvested, stored and owned by large companies. When Facebook, Instagram,, and Twitter sell this data to advertising companies — $44 billion a year — users get nothing in return except the free use of the social-media platform."[54]

Digi.me and factor.io are two of a dozen or so startups focused on creating solutions giving consumers control over their data. This includes the ability to sell or monetize their own data, giving the individual consumer a piece of the action. How this plays out in the world of retail and customer-identified purchase data is unknown, but it is easy to envision a scenario where the retailer owns the product data along with the ability to aggregate purchases to an ID, but the customer retains ownership of their identity. In this scenario the individual customer must give the retailer the right to access their data to market to them.

I can easily envision a day, probably sooner than later, when a forward-looking retailer, having a deep understanding of these issues, looks to partner with its customers, including sharing in the lucrative marketing funds that flow through the massive consumer goods industry. This is almost a natural evolution as we progress in the future of Retail in the Age of 'i'.

The Minority Report comes to Life

Some of you may recall Minority Report, a 2002 movie starring Tom Cruise. There is a scene in the movie where Cruise is walking through a shopping area and kiosks are identifying him in realtime through a biometric eye scan which triggers a personalized message. Many of the pieces required to bring this kind of scenario to life are actually being put in place today.

There are countless ways to recognize a shopper on his or her way in the entrance to the physical store. Facial recognition is being used extensively in other fields and anonymous facial recognition is already in retail. It's easy to connect a facial scan to a transaction at checkout, even without knowing the customer's name, thus being able to recognize that shopper again in the future. Alternatively, a notification can be sent to a shopper's mobile when the device is detected by a wireless network. That notification can ask for the shopper's ok to market to them individually.

Based on the OK, the retailer can connect in realtime to the shopper's personal data cloud, which contains key attributes and information informing the retailer of the individual shopper's brand preferences, allergies, interests, and more.

With that knowledge in hand, the retailer's marketing bot instantly peruses the products and services available at the store location, deciding which things to communicate to the customer who has just walked in the door.

New services like digi.me or factor.io can become one of the building blocks for the customer-based shopping experience in the Age of 'i'. Big data along with AI and machine learning capabilities will enable a world where a shopper can walk into any store, anywhere, and receive a personalized experience. The era of the 'smart' store is not far away.

CHAPTER 14

The Clock is Ticking

The $650 billion supermarket industry is rupturing in realtime as traditional competitors grow more aggressive, grocery buying moves online, technology-driven innovation explodes across the supply chain, consumers push back against packaged foods, and new competitors absorb industry sales growth. How bad is the carnage? An October 2017 Wall Street Journal article called out that while there were 25,380 grocery stores with at least $2 million in annual sales in 2016, only an estimated 19,000 will remain open by 2021. That's a decline of nearly 6,000 stores in the next few years.

When the dust clears, half of traditional grocery retailers may not be around."55

These forces are already being felt. Acting as an early warning system signaling the coming storm, the recent bankruptcies of regional retailers like Marsh, Tops Markets, and Southeastern Grocers are a precursor to the main event, their highly leveraged balance sheets a tripwire set off by the slightest tremors. As part of their Chapter 11 filing, Southeastern Grocers closed nearly 15% of its stores. Tops Markets closed 10 of its 169 stores under its filing, a number sure to increase.

Under growing pressure Supervalu sold itself to Unfi, the unconventional pairing a sign of the impending carnage. As part of the sale, Supervalu moved to quickly divest itself of remaining retail banners, bringing an abrupt end to an expensive foray outside its traditional wholesale business.

30% of Existing Supermarkets will be gone by 2025 - Tom Blischok

---

Showcasing the growing pressure on smaller operators, Martin's, a 21 store retailer in Michigan, recently announced it is being acquired by it's wholesaler, SpartanNash. This on top of another recent announcement that 17 store Best Markets is being acquired by Lidl. King Kullen, a 32 store retailer on Long Island has had enough and is selling itself to Ahold. And a growing number of small independent operators are simply closing their doors as the largest wholesalers roll up smaller distributors seeking to consolidate their positions. Case in point: The nation's largest wholesaler C&S Wholesale Grocery just announced it is acquiring Olean Wholesale. And all this is just a warmup to the main event as the industry prepares to shed thousands of brick and mortar stores over the next few years.

"$177b of U.S. online grocery sales will be done online by 2022, doubling this year's $88 billion. That's bigger than electronics and toys combined." - Cowen & Co.

In periodic calls I do with the Deutsche Bank research analyst team covering the supermarket industry, recent discussions have converged on the belief that the U.S. supermarket industry is going to look very different within the next few years as a major restructuring accelerates. Store closings will not be spread evenly across the industry players. The largest retailers like Walmart and Kroger are investing hundreds of millions of dollars each year as they attempt to keep pace with Amazon and other tech firms encroaching on their once secure domain. The increasing pace of innovation, and with it the need for retailers to discover, test, and deploy new capabilities, will put increasing pressure on resource constrained smaller retailers.

The large mid-market, populated by a surprising number of closely-held regional retailers, will be the industry's most active battlefield as retailers balance their historical strengths with shopper demand for new services and productivity gains realized by the biggest companies, all driven by sophisticated technologies.

"36% of FMCG retailers don't have a website or mobile app for online purchases" - Nielsen and FMI survey of brick & mortar retailers

This is not a 'wave' or a burst of frenzied innovation that will pass with time and everything returning to how it was. We have hit the point of inflection on the exponential growth curve and noticeable change will occur at a constantly increasing pace. As a recent report from McKinsey states: "Monumental forces are disrupting the industry. If grocers don't act, they'll be letting $200 billion to $700 billion in revenues shift to discount, online, and non-grocery channels and putting at risk more than $1 trillion in earnings before interest and taxes (EBIT). *When the dust clears, half of traditional grocery retailers may not be around.*"[56]

Retailers are struggling to keep pace with the shift online and their faster moving competitors. "Existing operations and legacy technology infrastructure pose a risk to companies that can't transform quickly enough to compete against companies that were "born digital," according to research conducted by North Carolina State University's Enterprise Risk Management Initiative and management consulting firm Protiviti Inc. This risk factor surged to the top spot for 2019, up from 10th place in the 2018 report."[57]

Clayton Christensen, author of the Innovator's Dilemma, has clearly identified the difficulty of creating disruptive innovation within an existing business. Owners and investors wish to protect the profitability of the status quo. Management, associates, and even customers like the safety and security of a world they know. And yet the historical retail strategy of being a 'fast follower' is a recipe for disaster in today's increasingly fast paced world. Retail in the Age of 'i' rewards speed and boldness, and punishes the slowness and safety of yesterday's approach.

> *"To put it another way: When faced with a competitor like Amazon, do you do as Walmart did, and invest heavily in tech firms and technical knowledge? Or do you go the way of Sears…into bankruptcy court?"58*

The clock is ticking and time is running out for retailers to ready themselves for Retail in the Age of 'i'. We are approaching day 12 in the lily pond and what we don't know we don't know is becoming very dangerous.

Chapter 15

Taking Action

Years ago, when I began traveling extensively, my first question when planning a trip was 'what's the cheapest fare?'. Travel was a cost of goods and I was after the lowest price available, regardless of the airline.

As time went along, I joined the various airline frequent flyer programs and began to accumulate more miles on American as they offered the most flights for where I was traveling. Within a short period, I had earned a free flight in American's program, lowering my cost of goods even more. Fabulous!

So I focused more of my travel on American to earn more free flights. And then something happened along the way. While I was focused on the economic benefit (free flights), I began moving up in the airline's program, receiving a growing number of services like early boarding, automatic rebooking, upgrades, and more.

The more I traveled, the more I came to appreciate those services. Today, I take for granted that if a flight is delayed or cancelled, American will automatically rebook me. I board early so I'm always assured of finding a space for my carryon. No matter where I'm sitting on the plane, the flight attendant addresses me by name.

Here's the point: When I go to travel now I no longer ask 'what'. Instead, I ask 'who', and the who is nearly always American Airlines.

Retailers inevitably focus on the 'what'. The 'what' being products. It is the sale of the 'what' that has driven retail for many decades now. What products will be promoted? What marketing and advertising vehicles do I use to promote the chosen products? What price will the product be promoted at?

But it doesn't stop there. Retail as an industry has organized itself around the 'what'. Category management was created in search of a better way to organize and promote the sale of products. Incentive programs based on the sale and profit margin of products have embedded this focus on the 'what' throughout the retail organization. Store and department managers are incentivized to control product shrink. And on and on.

And it gets worse. Decades of product-based mass promotion have trained shoppers to focus on the 'what'. What's the cheapest price on Tide laundry detergent this week?

I want to challenge your 'what' worldview. And suggest to you that in the Age of 'i', you need to ask the 'who'. And, more importantly, you want your shoppers to move from asking 'what' to asking 'who'. Who do I enjoy shopping with? Who knows me? Who makes me happy?

So how do you do this? How do you shift your worldview?

It happens inside the questions you ask. And the questions retailers need to be asking should flow from the questions that customers are asking about your retail operation. Today, retailers start from a product-based perspective and ask "What products should we put on the front page this week?" Instead, you as the retailer should be seeking to answer Sasha's question: "Who is going to provide me savings on the diapers I need to buy today?" And then the same question from each individual customer.

Succeeding as a retailer in the Age of 'i' is as simple, and as difficult, as that shift in worldview. It is understanding the power of that distinction, a product-based view of the world versus a customer-based view of the world, that opens up the future.

Let's use the five 'i' framework to help organize your thinking and activities as you move towards an iRetail future. Within each 'i' we're going to start with the question the customer is asking. Retailers have to work at stepping outside your usual comfort zone and really view the world from a customer's perspective.

Each customer question is then followed by five questions retailers need to be asking themselves around how they (the retailer) can answer the customer. The purpose of this exercise is to get retailers thinking about the capabilities needed as we move forward into the Age of 'i'.

Individual

The customer is asking: "Can you provide me savings on products I want to buy?"

Questions retailers need to ask themselves to identify required capabilities:

- Do you have the ability to understand what specific products are going to appeal to each individual customer next week? The week after that?
- Do you have the ability to personalize pricing to your individual customers?
- Do you have the ability to communicate customer-specific promotions to the individual customer?
- Do you have the ability to deliver customer-specific promotion pricing at checkout?
- Are your store associates able to recognize me when I'm in your store shopping? Can they provide me with information and services relevant to me?

Intelligence

The customer is asking: **"Do you know me?"**

Questions retailers need to ask themselves to identify required capabilities:

- Do you have customer identified purchase data along with scores and attributes derived from that purchase data such as brand propensity, discount propensity, purchase cadence, etc.?
- Does your product file have attributes for each product that can help in suggesting relevant products to the individual customer? This would include health related attributes (gluten-free, etc.), lifestyle attributes (like natural, organic or vegan), sustainability attributes, and more.
- Do you bring in third-party data, such as that from Experian or Acxiom, to help score share-of-wallet, and other customer attributes to power greater understanding and relevancy?
- Do you have location data, such as in-store realtime location of the customer so you're able to provide relevant information to the specific customer based on where he or she is in the store?
- Do you have awareness of your customer's health concerns? Such as if they are diabetic, have hypertension, are pregnant, or other conditions that are nutritionally sensitive?

Integrated Systems

The customer is asking: **"Do you make shopping easy and efficient for me?"**

Questions retailers need to ask themselves to identify required capabilities:

- Do you provide a seamless and cohesive customer user experience across your digital touchpoints?
- Can a customer create a shopping list and then choose to shop themselves or send it to your online shopping service for pickup or delivery?
- Is your store-level product category available to browse online without having to start an online shopping transaction?
- Can you tie product location to your mobile app to help customers sort their shopping list by aisle for the store they are in or navigate to the product they are seeking?
- Do you have realtime product inventory at the store level connected to your online shopping service to minimize online order substitutions?

Immersive Shopping

The customer is asking: "**Do you help me discover and learn about products relevant to me when I'm shopping in your stores and online?**"

Questions retailers need to ask themselves to identify required capabilities:

- Do your stores make shopping fun and interesting?
- Do you help customers discover relevant products throughout the shopping journey in the store and online?
- Do you help educate your customers about the products you sell? For example, helping the customer learn about the local farm growing strawberries, or featuring something like Harvest Market's micro-churnery and how the cream is used in the bakery and producing other products?
- Do you have any kind of digital in-store capabilities like kiosks or digital signage that can be used to convey relevant information like recipe suggestions or product information?
- Do you use augmented reality to enrich the shopping experience?

Innovation

The customer is asking: **"Do you use new tech capabilities to make shopping easier, provide more information on products, and guide me to products relevant and beneficial to me?"**

Questions retailers need to ask themselves to identify required capabilities:

- Do you have a formal innovation process to help your organization gain awareness of new capabilities entering the market?
- Do you budget for new innovation? Budgets for testing and trialing new capabilities across your organization?
- Do you have an innovation culture? Are your people truly open to new innovation or do they find it threatening?
- How do you break the typical logjam that quickly occurs when trying to grow your organization's ability to implement a growing number of new capabilities?
- Are you pursuing developing an agile philosophy throughout your organization?

Now let's move from questions to insights and action. Under each of the 'i' sections, give yourself one point for each 'yes' answer you have for each of the five questions. So you can have a maximum of five points for each 'i'.

Using the iRetail scorecard, color in the number of points ('yes' answers) you have for each of the 'i' sections. So you have something that looks like the example below.

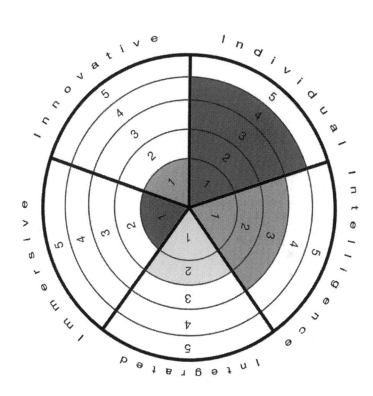

This radar map represents your existing capabilities, as represented by the shaded area. The remaining unshaded area represents the gaps you have relative to iRetail capabilities.

The gaps should serve to point you towards new capabilities needed to address the customer's needs for that 'i' area, effectively creating a roadmap for needed solutions and gives you a place to look for new innovation. You can also go through this exercise scoring your competitors, providing you some sense of how you compare in the marketplaces you serve.

This is a simplified example of a far more detailed and comprehensive methodology developed by CART to help retailers in their journey into the Age of 'i'. A deep dive into a retailer's existing and planned systems identifies existing capabilities that are then aligned to the needs of each area, the result being a detailed gap analysis.

The gap analysis in turn drives the creation of a detailed roadmap, calling out in a prioritized order, the needed capabilities that need to be researched, identified, and deployed.

The gap analysis and roadmap are the first two steps in the retailer's journey into the Age of 'i', a journey that consists of five parts:

1. Understanding your capability gap: As you can begin to grasp from the questions above, there are countless details that vary across retailers that define existing capabilities. The process can begin with an intense fact-finding related to systems and processes used by your organization today alongside an understanding of what's needed to truly focus on each individual customer.

2. Creating a roadmap: Using the knowledge gained from understanding existing capabilities and the associated gaps, create a roadmap to guide your efforts, a step-by-step path to the iRetail future. Admittedly, this can be challenging given the interplay between the five 'i's, such as how does intelligence inform the ability to make an immersive shopping experience relevant to the individual customer? The secret is using the individual customer as your beacon, aligning everything to that focus.

3. Putting in place a formal innovation program to address the gaps: The initial focus of a formalized innovation program is to help you fill the gaps and address the needed capabilities you've identified in the roadmap. As we've seen, the pace of innovation grows daily and there is a continual flood of new solutions available to address the applicable capability gaps. And beyond the immediate roadmap, innovation is occurring at an ever-growing pace that will continually expand your ability to focus on the individual customer. Make sure that you are working to maximize your view to new innovation on an ongoing basis.

4. Building an iRetail culture: From our experience there are two pieces to this. The first is working to get your executive team, followed by more of your organization, open to new innovation. We have found that the ability of an organization to be open to new possibility and new ways of doing things is more important than what resources are available.

5. Making your organization Agile: Beyond creating a culture of innovation is giving your organization the ability and flexibility to move faster so you are able to keep pace with changes happening in the marketplace. Agile is a project management philosophy often used in software development, that is characterized by dividing tasks into short bursts of work, along with frequent communication to constantly reassess and adapt. The Agile movement is increasingly being applied to organizations as a way to help companies adapt and succeed in the new world of ever-faster change and disruption.

A friend, having read a draft of this book, commented that while everything presented is spot-on, the journey to an iRetail future is not an easy one for traditional retailers to embark upon. He called out the impact across the many operational areas and activities alongside the ever-changing marketplace and innovation that is occurring. His straightforward directive for retailers is simple: GET STARTED!

<small>CHAPTER 16</small>

Conclusion

So we now live in a world where the increasing pace of tech-fueled transformation creates a chaotic environment for retail, a world where we don't know what we don't know. And where what we don't know can upend even the most successful companies. How do retail executives operate in such a world? How is planning done, the budgeting and allocation of finite resources? Building and renovating stores in the physical world requires planning and time horizons sometimes measured in years. Unlike the digital world, the physical world comes with many constraints.

We need a way to bring order to the chaos, a beacon to fix upon and navigate through the growing storm. That beacon is the customer. And not just 'the customer' generically, but *each individual customer* you have shopping with you. As we proceed along the ever-rising growth curve of technology, five-year business plans become less and less reliable as we increasingly don't know what what's coming next. But there remains one constant in retail: The customer.

Retail in the Age of 'i' is intended to challenge the retail industry to think differently; to shift focus from selling products to instead nurturing customers. In the torrent of disruption sweeping today's retail industry there is no room for anything less than a laser focus on each and every customer.

Retailers have a unique opportunity to truly partner with each of their customers as we move forward. The ability to create and foster relationships, facilitated by technology, but accomplished by people, provides immense opportunity for those who get it right. There is no end to this journey, our customers, technologies, indeed the world, are constantly changing and evolving.

The retail industry has available to it technologies and capabilities never before possible. Retailers can either continue to follow, unwilling to accept the yoke of innovation, or they can jump into the game and create the future.

Welcome to Retail in the Age of 'i'.

"You cannot escape the responsibility of tomorrow by evading it today."
- Abraham Lincoln

About the Author

Gary Hawkins has led customer-focused innovation across fast moving consumer goods retail for over twenty years. As a retailer he pioneered one of the first loyalty programs in U.S. supermarket retail, driving early insights to true shopping behavior and customer-level economics. As a strategic advisor to prominent retailers and brand manufacturers around the world, Hawkins led development of collaborative marketing initiatives leveraging customer data, laying the foundation for the shopper marketing movement. Parlaying an early view to new technologies, Hawkins and his team developed the first personalized marketing capability for mass retail over a decade ago.

Today, as Founder and CEO of CART (the Center for Advancing Retail & Technology), Gary Hawkins has an unparalleled view to current and future innovation in fast moving consumer goods retail. CART sits at the epicenter of retail transformation as his team connects retailers to new innovation using a vast network to understand the challenges and opportunities facing retailers, wholesalers, brand manufacturers, and solution providers. Reviewing hundreds of new solutions each year, combined with years of industry experience, uniquely position Hawkins to guide retail into the future.

Hawkins uses his ability to distill the complexity of technology-fueled retail innovation into actionable insights which he shares as a strategist, author, and noted speaker at industry events worldwide. He has authored two internationally published books, numerous white papers, myriad articles, and is an oft-quoted resource for numerous publications. Hawkins is a regular guest lecturer at Georgetown University's McDonough School of Business in addition to keynoting retail conferences in the US and abroad.

[1] Rose, Marina. "The Science Of Human Connection And Wellness In A Digitally Connected World." Medium.com. https://medium.com/thrive-global/the-science-of-human-connection-and-wellness-in-a-digitally-connected-world-611eb8c1b51c (accessed February 2, 2019).

[2] Kerrigan, S.J. "Exponential Growth and the Inevitable Collapse of Medicare Explained." Seankerrigan.com. http://seankerrigan.com/exponential-growth-collapse-medicare-explained/ (accessed February 2, 2019).

[3] Gent, Edd. "IBM's New Computer Is the Size of a Grain of Salt and Costs Less than 10 Cents." Singularityhub.com. https://singularityhub.com/2018/03/26/ibms-new-computer-is-the-size-of-a-grain-of-salt-and-costs-less-than-10-cents/#sm.000ubpi0s1ad1e7psxn2jl9rj42u5 (accessed February 2, 2019).

[4] Watkins, Steve. "'Bananacam,' ClickList improvements among innovations Kroger's technology unit is launching". bizjournals.com. https://www.bizjournals.com/cincinnati/news/2017/02/13/exclusive-bananacam-clicklist-improvements-among.html (accessed Feb 2, 2019).

[5] Molla, Rani. "Amazon spent nearly $23 billion on R&D last year - more than any other U.S. company.' recode.net. https://www.recode.net/2018/4/9/17204004/amazon-research-development-rd (accessed February 2, 2019).

[6] Buzek, Greg. "Amazon Has A TIGIR By The Tail." ihlservices.com. https://www.ihlservices.com/news/analyst-corner/2017/01/amazon-has-a-tigir-by-the-tail/ (accessed February 2, 2019).

[7] Petro, Greg. "Build It Or Buy It: Will Amazon Or Walmart Win The Retail Innovation Battle?" forbes.com. https://www.forbes.com/sites/gregpetro/2018/07/01/build-it-or-buy-it-will-amazon-or-walmart-win-the-retail-innovation-battle/#30b7ed47501d (accessed February 2, 2019).

[8] Perez, Sarah. "Voice shopping estimated to hit $40+ billion across U.S. and U.K. by 2022." techcrunch.com.

https://techcrunch.com/2018/03/02/voice-shopping-estimated-to-hit-40-billion-across-u-s-and-u-k-by-2022/ (accessed February 2, 2019).

[9] Kharpal, Arjun. "Amazon's voice assistant Alexa could be a $10 billion 'mega-hit' by 2020: Research." CNBC.com. https://www.cnbc.com/2017/03/10/amazon-alexa-voice-assistan-could-be-a-10-billion-mega-hit-by-2020-research.html (accessed February 2, 2019).

[10] Diamandis, Peter. "The Spatial Web Will Map Our 3D World - And Change Everything In the Process." singularityhub.com. https://singularityhub.com/2018/11/16/the-spatial-web-will-map-our-3d-world-and-change-everything-about-it-in-the-process/#sm.00000pe6xkqndadvgy6agwmm5zajv (accessed February 2, 2019).

[11] March 2018 Progressive Grocer Market Research; The Super 50

[12] Mims, Christopher. "Every Company Is Now a Tech Company." WSJ.com. https://www.wsj.com/articles/every-company-is-now-a-tech-company-1543901207?mod=hp_jr_pos3 (accessed February 2, 2019).

[13] Watkins, Steve. "Dillon retiring from Kroger board." bizjournals.com. https://www.bizjournals.com/cincinnati/news/2014/12/11/former-ceo-dillon-retiring-from-kroger.html (accessed February 2, 2019).

[14] Marcarelli, Rebekah. "Kroger's Private Brands Seeing 'Remarkable' Success, Says CEO." winsightgrocerybusiness.com. https://www.winsightgrocerybusiness.com/retailers/krogers-private-brands-seeing-remarkable-success-says-ceo (accessed February 2, 2019).

[15] Danziger, Pamela. "How Amazon Plans To Dominate The Private Label Market." forbes.com https://www.forbes.com/sites/pamdanziger/2018/05/06/how-amazon-plans-to-dominate-the-private-label-market/#21c12f8072d9 (accessed February 2, 2019).

[16] Hamstra, Mark. "Amazon tallies $10M in Whole Foods 365 private label sales." supermarketnews.com.

https://www.supermarketnews.com/private-label/amazon-tallies-10m-whole-foods-365-private-label-sales (accessed February 2, 2019).

[17] "Shopper Marketing Definition." shoppermarketingmag.com. https://shoppermarketingmag.com/shopper-marketing-definition (accessed February 2, 2019).

[18] Tenser, James. "Kraft Heinz Aims to Create Growth through Digital Transformation." cpgmatters.com. http://www.cpgmatters.com/DigitalSolutions120318.html (accessed February 2, 2019).

[19] Kestenbaum, Richard. "Your Friend May Pay Less Than You For The Same Things You're Buying." forbes.com. https://www.forbes.com/sites/richardkestenbaum/2018/07/30/your-friend-may-pay-less-than-you-for-the-same-things-youre-buying/#2914a9ac1c8c (accessed February 2, 2019).

[20] Columbus, Louis. "10 Charts That Will Change Your Perspective Of Big Data's Growth." forbes.com. https://www.forbes.com/sites/louiscolumbus/2018/05/23/10-charts-that-will-change-your-perspective-of-big-datas-growth/#29adb8f82926 (accessed February 2, 2019).

[21] Gunst, Carole. "10 Eye-opening Stats About the Growth of Big Data." attunity.com. https://www.attunity.com/blog/10-eye-opening-stats-about-the-growth-of-big-data/ (accessed February 2, 2019).

[22] Paul, Kari. "Americans' data is worth billions - and you soon might be able to get a cut of it." marketwatch.com https://www.marketwatch.com/story/americans-data-is-worth-billions-and-you-soon-might-be-able-to-get-a-cut-of-it-2018-10-09?ns=prod/accounts-mw&ns=prod/accounts-mw (accessed February 2, 2019).

[23] Goad, Nick. "Use Big Data to Give Local Shoppers What They Want." bcg.com. https://www.bcg.com/en-us/publications/2018/use-big-data-give-local-shoppers-what-they-want.aspx (accessed February 2, 2019).

[24] Sopadjieva, Emma. "A Study of 46,000 Shoppers Shows That Omnichannel Retailing Works." https://hbr.org/2017/01/a-study-of-46000-shoppers-shows-that-omnichannel-retailing-works (accessed February 2, 2019).

[25] "The Grocery Digital Divide." Deloitte Consulting (accessed February 2, 2019).

[26] Georgiou, Michael. "User Experience Is the Most Important Metric You Aren't Measuring." entrepeneur.com. https://www.entrepreneur.com/article/309161 (accessed February 2, 2019).

[27] Peranzo, Pete. "7 Reasons People Leave Your Website." imaginovation.net. https://www.imaginovation.net/blog/7-reasons-people-leave-your-website/ (accessed February 2, 2019).

[28] Moth, David. "Site speed: case studies, tips and tools for improving your conversion rate." econsultancy.com. https://econsultancy.com/site-speed-case-studies-tips-and-tools-for-improving-your-conversion-rate/ (accessed February 2, 2019).

[29] Hogan, Andrew. "The Six Steps For Justifying Better UX." forrester.com. https://www.forrester.com/report/The+Six+Steps+For+Justifying+Better+UX/-/E-RES117708 (accessed February 2, 2019).

[30] "U.S. Consumers Take an Omnichannel Approach When It Comes to Grocery Shopping." npd.com. https://www.npd.com/wps/portal/npd/us/news/press-releases/2018/us-consumers-take-an-omnichannel-approach-when-it-comes-to-grocery-shopping/ (accessed February 2, 2019).

[31] Abramovich, Giselle. "The 5 Biggest Marketing Trends For 2019." cmo.com. https://www.cmo.com/features/articles/2018/12/12/the-5-biggest-marketing-trends-for-2019.html#gs.kEw61BNp (accessed February 2, 2019).

[32] Taylor, Kate. "Almost half of millennials say they'd rather give up sex than quit Amazon for a year, according to a new survey." businessinsider.com. https://www.businessinsider.com/millennials-pick-amazon-over-sex-survey-2018-12 (accessed February 2, 2019).

[33] Vincent, Roger. "Century City mall goes deluxe with $1-billion makeover to entice online shoppers." latimes.com. https://www.latimes.com/business/la-fi-century-city-mall-20170927-story.html (accessed February 2, 2019).

[34] Springer, Jon. "Made From Scratch: Harvest Market." winsightgrocerybusiness.com. https://www.winsightgrocerybusiness.com/equipment-design/made-scratch-harvest-market. (accessed February 2, 2019).

[35] www.projectnourished.com (accessed February 2, 2019).

[36] Abramovich, Giselle. "The 5 Biggest Marketing Trends For 2019." cmo.com. https://www.cmo.com/features/articles/2018/12/12/the-5-biggest-marketing-trends-for-2019.html#gs.kEw61BNp (accessed February 2, 2019).

[37] Rogers, Sol. "Why Retailers Are Using VR & AR To Get The Competitive Edge At Christmas." forbes.com. https://www.forbes.com/sites/solrogers/2018/11/08/why-retailers-are-using-vr-ar-to-get-the-competitive-edge-at-christmas/#7f57fadc61b3 (accessed February 2, 2019).

[38] Knutson, Emma Grace. "New Trends in Grocery Shopping." millennialmagazine.com. https://millennialmagazine.com/2017/05/28/new-trends-in-grocery-shopping/ (accessed February 2, 2019).

[39] Frank, Aaron. "Inside a $1 billion Real Estate Company Operating Entirely in VR." singularityhub.com. https://singularityhub.com/2018/07/08/inside-a-1-billion-real-estate-company-operating-entirely-in-vr/#sm.000ubpi0s1ad1e7psxn2jl9rj42u5 (accessed February 2, 2019).

[40] Nichols, Greg. "Walmart gives employees VR combat training for holiday rush." zdnet.com. https://www.zdnet.com/article/walmart-giving-employees-vr-combat-training-for-holiday-rush/ (accessed February 2, 2019).

[41] Moon, Mariella. "Walmart turns to VR and Oculus Go for associates' training." engadget.com.

https://www.engadget.com/2018/09/20/walmart-vr-training-oculus-go/ (accessed February 2, 2019).

[42] "CMS: US health care spending to reach nearly 20% of GDP by 2025." advisory.com. https://www.advisory.com/daily-briefing/2017/02/16/spending-growth (accessed February 2, 2019).

[43] Stobbe, Mike. "U.S. life expectancy declines again in sobering 'wake-up call'." statnews.com. https://www.statnews.com/2018/11/29/u-s-life-expectancy-declines-again-in-sobering-wake-up-call/ (accessed February 2, 2019).

[44] Dolan, Shelagh. "Three untapped opportunities wearables present to health insurers, providers, and employers." businessinsider.com. https://www.businessinsider.com/wearables-in-healthcare-b-2018-8 (accessed February 2, 2019).

[45] Khullar, Dhruv. "Do You Trust the Medical Profession?". nytimes.com. https://www.nytimes.com/2018/01/23/upshot/do-you-trust-the-medical-profession.html (accessed February 2, 2019).

[46] Stern, Joanna. "Tech That Will Change Your Life in 2019." wsj.com. https://www.wsj.com/articles/tech-that-will-change-your-life-in-2019-11546092180 (accessed February 2, 2019).

9 Thomas, Nick. "PayThink Digital identity control belongs in the hands of the consumer." paymentssource.com. https://www.paymentssource.com/opinion/new-identity-technology-should-give-consumers-more-control (accessed February 2, 2019).

[48] Isaac, Mike. "Facebook Security Breach Exposes Accounts of 50 Million Users." nytimes.com. https://www.nytimes.com/2018/09/28/technology/facebook-hack-data-breach.html (accessed February 2, 2019).

[49] Sterling, Greg. "Pew survey finds marked decline in Facebook user engagement since March." marketingland.com. https://marketingland.com/pew-survey-finds-marked-decline-in-facebook-user-engagement-since-march-247469 (accessed February 2, 2019).

[50] Valentino-DeVries, Jennifer. "Your Apps Know Where You Were Last Night, and They're Not Keeping It Secret. nytimes.com. https://www.nytimes.com/interactive/2018/12/10/business/location-data-privacy-apps.html (accessed February 2, 2019).

[51] "Ad Blocking User Penetration Rate in the United States from 2014 to 2018." statista.com. https://www.statista.com/statistics/804008/ad-blocking-reach-usage-us/ (accessed February 2, 2019).

[52] Britton, Katherine. "IoT Big Data: Consumer Wearables Data Privacy and Security." americanbar.com. https://www.americanbar.org/publications/landslide/2015-16/november-december/IoT-Big-Data-Consumer-Wearables-Data-Privacy-Security/ (accessed February 2, 2019).

[53] Sterling, Greg. "Survey shows US ad-blocking usage is 40 percent on laptops, 15 percent on mobile." marketingland.com. https://marketingland.com/survey-shows-us-ad-blocking-usage-40-percent-laptops-15-percent-mobile-216324 (accessed February 2, 2019).

[54] Paul, Kari. "Americans' data is worth billions - and you soon might be able to get a cut of it." marketwatch.com https://www.marketwatch.com/story/americans-data-is-worth-billions-and-you-soon-might-be-able-to-get-a-cut-of-it-2018-10-09?ns=prod/accounts-mw&ns=prod/accounts-mw (accessed February 2, 2019).

[55] Kuijpers, Dymfke. "Reviving grocery retail: Six imperatives." mckinsey.com. https://www.mckinsey.com/industries/retail/our-insights/reviving-grocery-retail-six-imperatives (accessed February 2, 2019).

[56] Kuijpers, Dymfke. "Reviving grocery retail: Six imperatives." mckinsey.com. https://www.mckinsey.com/industries/retail/our-insights/reviving-grocery-retail-six-imperatives (accessed February 2, 2019).

[57] Sun, Mengqi. "Businesses Predict Digital Transformation to Be Biggest Risk Factor in 2019." blogs.wsj.com. https://blogs.wsj.com/riskandcompliance/2018/12/05/businesses-

predict-digital-transformation-to-be-biggest-risk-factors-in-2019/?guid=BL-252B-15931&mod=hp_minor_pos10&dsk=y (accessed February 2, 2019).

[58] Mims, Christopher. "Every Company is now a Tech Company". https://www.wsj.com/articles/every-company-is-now-a-tech-company-1543901207?mod=hp_jr_pos3. (accessed February 2, 2019).

Made in the USA
Lexington, KY
25 October 2019